Charles Reade

Singleheart and Doubleface

A Matter-Of-Fact Romance

Charles Reade

Singleheart and Doubleface
A Matter-Of-Fact Romance

ISBN/EAN: 9783744666329

Printed in Europe, USA, Canada, Australia, Japan

Cover: Foto ©Thomas Meinert / pixelio.de

More available books at **www.hansebooks.com**

SINGLEHEART AND DOUBLEFACE

A MATTER-OF-FACT ROMANCE

BY

CHARLES READE, D.C.L.

London
CHATTO & WINDUS, PICCADILLY
1884

SINGLEHEART AND DOUBLEFACE.

CHAPTER I.

MATTHEW BRENT, a small shopkeeper in Green Street, Liverpool, was a widower with two daughters. Deborah, the elder, had plenty of tongue and mother-wit, but could not and would not study anything on earth if it had the misfortune to be written or printed. Sarah, the younger, showed attention and application from her childhood.

Her father cultivated those powers, for they are the roots of all excellence, and he knew it. He sent the girl to school, and there she learned the usual smattering; and one thing worth it all, viz., how to teach herself. Under that abler tuition she learned to write like a clerk, to keep her father's books, to remember the price of every article in the shop, to serve the customers when required, and to read for her own pleasure and instruction. At eighteen she was Brent's right hand all day, and his reader at night.

Deborah, who could only spell *The Mercury*, and would not do that if she could get Sally to read it out, found her level as cook, housekeeper, and market-woman. At twenty she was very tall, supple, and muscular; comely, but freckled, reddish hair, a very white skin, only it tanned easily. It revealed its natural beauty in her throat, and above all in the nape of her neck. This nape, snowy and solid, and a long row of ivory teeth, were her beauties. She married quite young her father's cousin, a small farmer, and settled in Berkshire, her native county.

Sarah Brent was about two inches shorter than Deborah, but a finer figure; had an oval face full of modesty and gentle dignity. Her skin was also white, and revealed itself in her shapely hands as well as her alabaster throat.

Her hair was brown, and so were two fearless eyes that looked at people full without staring. When she was nineteen, a worthy young fellow, called Joseph Pinder, fell in love with her and courted her. He was sheepish and distant in his approaches, for he looked on her as a superior being. She never chattered, yet could always answer civilly and wisely; this, and her Madonna-like face, made Joe Pinder reverence her. Her father thought highly of him, and connived at his visits, and so they were often seen together in a friendly way; but when he began to make downright love to her, she told him calmly she could go no farther than friendship. 'And indeed,' said she, 'I would never leave my father for any young man.'

Joseph Pinder knew that this declaration has often preceded connubial rites, and continued his friendly assiduities; and these two often came back from church together, he glowing with delight at being near her, and she cool and friendly.

The Brents were in a small way of business,

and Sarah's adorer was a decorative painter, and what is called in the trade a 'writer'—one of those astounding artists who by skilful shading make gilt letters appear concave, or convex, or-stand out bodily from a board or wall, and blazon a shopkeeper's name and business. On one occasion he had a large job of this sort to do in Manchester. It took him a fortnight, and led to another at Preston. In a month he came back with money in both pockets, and full of joy at the prospect of meeting Sarah again.

He found the Brents at supper, and there was a young man with them who had a deal to say, and made the old man smile, while the young woman often looked furtively at him with undisguised complacency. This was a second cousin of Mr. Brent's, one James Mansell, a painter and grainer, who had settled in the town while Pinder was away.

Pinder's heart sank at this, and instead of exerting himself in vigorous competition, he became more silent and more depressed the more James Mansell rattled away; in short, he was no company at all, because the other was good company.

After a while he said 'Good-night.'

A coquette would have followed him to the door and smoothed matters; but that was not Sarah Brent's line; she said 'Good-night' kindly enough, but she never moved, and James Mansell's tongue resumed its headlong course.

This was the first of many such scenes. Sarah was always kind, but cool, to her old admirer, and manifestly attracted by the new one. Indeed, it came to this at last that Pinder could never get a walk with her alone except from church.

On one occasion he ventured on a mild remonstrance : ' If you had not told me you would never leave your father, I should be almost afraid *that* James Mansell would entice you away from us all.'

'From everybody else; but not from father.'

One would think that was plain enough, but Joe could not realize it, and he went on to ask her if she could really find it in her heart to throw such an old friend as him over for a stranger.

She replied, calmly : ' Am I changed to you any way?   I always respected you, and I respect you still.'

' That is a comfort, Sarah.   But if this goes on, I'm afraid you will like another man far better than me, whether you respect me or not.'

' That is my business,' said she, firmly.

' Isn't it mine, too, Sarah?   We have kept company this two years.'

' As friends ; but nothing more.   I have never misled you, but now if you are wise you will take up with some other girl.   You can find as good as me.'

' Not in this world.'

' Nonsense, Joe ; and besides—— '

' Well, what ? '

' I am one that forecasts a little, and I am

afraid you will tease me, and pain yourself, and
some day we shall part bad friends, and that
would be a pity, after all.'

' Nothing but death shall part us.'

' Yes, this door will. Father is not well to-
night.' The door in question was the side door
of her own house.

Pinder took the hint, and bade her ' Good-
night' affectionately.

He walked a little way out into the country
by himself, wondering now whether she would
ever be his. He was dejected, but not in despair. In his class of life men and women
have often two or three warmish courtships before they marry. Sarah was not of that sort,
but this James Mansell would be as likely as
not to leave the town, and think no more of
Sarah Brent. In his trade it was here to-day
and there to-morrow, and he did not look like
the man to cling to the absent.

Pinder returned home by Green Street to
have a last look at the shell which held his pearl.
As he passed by on the other side of the

way, James Mansell came and knocked at Mr.
Brent's side door. Pinder waited with a certain
degree of jealous malice to see him excluded.
Sarah came to the door and parleyed; probably she told him her father was unwell.
Pinder went on a little way, and then turned
to see.

The colloquy continued. It seemed inter-
minable. The woman he loved was in no
hurry now to get back to her sick father, and
when she did, what was the result? Mansell
was invited in, after all, and the door of heaven
closed upon him instead of in his face.

The watcher stood there transfixed with
the poisoned arrow of jealousy. He was sick
and furious by turns, and at last got frightened
at himself, and resolved to keep out of the
way of this James Mansell, with whom he had
no chance, Sarah's preference was now so
clear.

But he was too much in love to forego the
walks from church; and Sarah never objected
to his company, nor, indeed, to his coming in

to supper afterward. But he was sure to find his rival there and be reduced to a sullen cipher.

So things went on. He did not see what passed between Mansell and Sarah Brent, the open wooing of the man, the timid tumult in the woman, expanding, ripening, blushing, thrilling, and blooming in the new sunshine. But he discovered a good deal; she seemed gliding gradually away from him down a gentle but inexorable slope. She was as friendly in her cool way as ever, but scarcely attended to him. Her mind seemed elsewhere at times, even in that short walk from church, sole relic now of their languid but unbroken friendship.

The time came when even this privilege was disputed. One Sunday James Mansell arrived in Green Street earlier than usual. He heard where Sarah was, so he came to meet her. She was walking with Pinder. Mansell had been drinking a little, and did not know perhaps how little cause he had for jealousy. He stepped rudely in between Pinder and Miss

Breut, and took her arm, whereas Pinder had been walking merely by her side.

'What sort of manners are these?' said Pinder.

'They are my manners,' said the other haughtily. 'She has no business to walk with you at all.'

'Don't insult *her*, at all events. She has walked with me this two year.'

'Well, then, now you go and walk with some other girl.'

'Not at your bidding, you brute.'.

'Oh, you want a hiding, do you?'

'No; it is you that want that.'

James Mansell replied by a blow, which took Pinder unawares, and sent him staggering.

He would have followed it up, but Pinder stopped the second neatly, and gave him a smart one in return, crying 'Coward! to take a man unawares.' Sarah was terrified, and clasped her hands. 'Oh, pray do not quarrel about *me*!'

'Stand aloof,' said Mansell, imperiously.

' This must end.' Sarah obeyed the man, who was evidently her master, but implored him not to hurt Joe Pinder ; he was only a friend. The truth is, Mansell had recounted such deeds of prowess that, what with his gasconades and her blind love, she thought no man could have a chance with him.

He sparred well, and hit Pinder several times, but rather short.

Both were soon infuriated, and they were all over the street, fighting and raging.

Under similar circumstances Virgil's heifer browsed the grass in undisturbed tranquillity, content to know that her mate would be the best bull of the two.

Not so Sarah Brent. She clasped her hands and screamed, and implored her hero to be merciful. Her conscience whispered that her inoffensive friend was being hardly used in every way.

Presently her hero, after administering several blows, and making his adversary bleed, received a left-handed stinger that made him

recoil. Maddened by this, he rushed at Pinder
to annihilate him. But Pinder was no novice
either; he drew back on the point of his toe,
and met James Mansell's rush with a tremendous slogger that sounded like a falling plank,
and shot him to the earth at Sarah Brent's very
feet, a distance of some yards.

All was changed in a moment; she literally
bounded over the prostrate form, and stood
between him and danger; for in Liverpool
they fight up and down, as the saying is. ' You
wretch,' she cried, ' to kill the man I love!'
It was Pinder's turn to stagger before that
white cheek, and those fiery eyes, and that
fatal word.

' Man you love ? ' said he.

' I love!—I love!—I love!' cried she,
stabbing with swift feminine instinct the monster
who had struck her Love.

Then Pinder fell back, subdued, with a sigh
of despair; she flung herself down, and raised
James Mansell's head and sobbed hysterically
over it.

Some people now came up ; but Pinder in those few seconds had undergone a change. He stepped forward, thrust the people away, and kneeling down, lifted James Mansell up and took him under his arm. 'Leave him to me, Sarah,' said he.

'To you?' she sobbed.

'Ay : do you think I shall ever hurt him again, now you have told me you love him?' And he said it so finely she knew he meant it. Then he sent to the market public-house for a sponge and some brandy, and meantime Mansell, who was tough, came to of himself; but the water and brandy completed his restoration to society. It was Pinder who sponged his face and nostrils, and took him to Brent's house, Sarah hovering near all the time like a hen over her chickens. She whipped into the house with her pass-key, and received her favourite at the door, then closed it gently, but decidedly: not that Joe Pinder would have come in if she had asked him. He did not even trust himself to say 'Good-night.' It was

all over between him and her, and of course
he knew it.

When she had got James Mansell safe she
made him lie down on the little sofa, and sat at
his head, applying cool linen rags to his swollen
cheeks and a cut upon his forehead due to
Pinder's knuckles,

Presently her father came in from visiting
a sick friend, and at sight of this group asked
what was to do.

' It is that cruel Joe Pinder been beating
him, father ; I thought he had killed him.'

' What for ? '

Sarah blushed and was silent ; she wouldn't
own that James was the aggressor, and yet she
wouldn't tell a falsehood.

' Joe Pinder ! ' said the old man.   ' He was
never quarrelsome ; there's not a better-hearted
young man in the town, nor a more respectable.
Now you tell me what was the quarrel about ? '

' Oh, father ! ' said Sarah, deprecatingly.

' Ay ! ay ! I needn't ask,' said the old man.
' It was about a woman, eh ?   You might have

been better employed, *all three*, this Sabbath evening.'

' Well, sir, Sarah was only coming home from church this Sabbath evening,' said Mansell ; ' but as for me, I was as much to blame as the other, so let us say no more about it.' Sarah whispered ' You are very generous.' The subject dropped till the old man retired to rest, and then James Mansell, who had been brooding, delivered himself thus : ' He is not half a bad sort that Joe Pinder. But he is one too many for me, or I am one too many for him, so you must make up your mind this night which is to be your husband, and give the other the sack.'

This was virile, and entitled to a feminine reply. It came immediately, in what, perhaps, if we could know the truth, is a formula—not a word, not even a syllable, but a white wrist passed round the neck, and a fair head deposited like down upon the shoulder of her conqueror.

Joseph Pinder grieved and watched, but

troubled the lovers no more. James Mansell pressed Sarah to name the day. She objected. Her father's health was breaking, and she would not leave him. Mansell urged her ; she stood firm. He accused her of not loving him; she sighed and wondered he could say that, but was immovable.

By-and-by it all came to her father's ears. He sent for a lawyer directly, and made the shop and house over to Sarah by deed of gift. Then he told her she need not wait for his death : he would prefer to see her happy with the man of her choice, and also to advise her in business for the little while he had to live.

So the banns were cried, and Joseph Pinder heard in silence; and in due course James Mansell was united to Sarah Brent in holy matrimony.

In its humble way this was a promising union. The man was twenty-seven, the woman twenty, and thoughtful beyond her years.

They had health and love and occupation ; moreover, the man's work took him out of the woman's way, except at meals, and in the evening. Now nothing sweetens married life and divests it of monotony and *ennui* more than these daily partings and meetings. Mansell had three trades, and in one of them, graining, he might be called an artist. He could imitate the common woods better than almost anybody ; but at satin-wood, mahogany, and American birch he was really wonderful. Sarah was a first-rate shop-woman, civil, prompt, obliging, and handsome — qualities that all attract in business. She gave no credit beyond a week, and took none at all.

In any class of life it is a fine thing when both spouses can contribute a share to the joint income. This is one of the boons found oftenest among the middle classes. Most labourers' wives can only keep house, and few gentlemen's wives can earn a penny.

The Mansells, then, upon a large and wide survey of life, were in a happy condition—

happier far than any pair who do not earn
their living.

One day a great sorrow came, but not un-
expectedly. Matthew Brent died peacefully,
blessing his daughters and his son-in-law.

The next day came a joyful event, Sarah's
child was born—a lovely girl.

Mighty nature comforted the bereaved
daughter, and soon the home was as cheerful
as ever.

Indeed, it was not till the third year of
her marriage that a cloud appeared, and that
seemed a small one, no bigger than a man's
hand.

James Mansell began to come home Saturday night instead of Saturday afternoon; and
the reason was clear, he smelt of liquor, and
though always sober, his speech was thick
on these occasions.

Sarah, who had forecasts, was alarmed, and
spoke in time. She remembered something
her father—an observant man—had said to her
in his day, viz., that your clever specimens

of the class which may be called artist-mechanics are often addicted to liquor.

However, this prudent woman thought it best not to raise an argument about drink; she merely represented to her husband that there was now a run upon her shop Saturday after-noon and evening, and really it was more than she could manage without his assistance; would he be so good as to help her? He assisted readily enough, and then the Saturday after-noons became her happiest time. He himself seemed to enjoy the business and the bustle and his wife's company.

But by-and-by he came home very late on Monday, with the usual signs of a drop; then she advised him and entreated him, but never scolded him. He acquiesced and was perfectly good-tempered, though in the wrong. But one day in the week he would come home late, and mumble what is called the Queen's English, but I believe the people hold a few shares in it. Sarah was disappointed, and a little alarmed, but began to hope it would go

no farther at all events.   However, one Saturday, if you please, he did not come to help her
in the shop, did not even come home to supper,
and she had made such a nice supper for him.
She sat at the window and fretted, she went
from the window to her sleeping child and
back again, restless and apprehensive.

At midnight, when the whole street was
still, footsteps rang on the pavement. She
looked out and saw two men, each with an
arm under the shoulder of a third, hoisting him
along. She darted to the street door, and
received her husband from the hands of two
men, who were perfectly sober.   One of them
turned on his heel and walked swiftly away at
sight of her.   But she saw him—for the first
time this three years.

It was Joseph Pinder.

CHAPTER II.

MR. MANSELL began his bibulous career with a redeeming quality more common in Russia than in England—good-natured in his cups. He chuckled feebly, and opposed the inertia of matter only, whilst the dismayed wife pulled him and pushed him, and at last got him down on the little sofa in the shop-parlour. Then she whipped off his necktie, and washed his face in diluted lavender-water, and put her salts to his nose. Being now on his back, he soon went to sleep and breathed sonorously, whilst she sat in her father's arm-chair and watched him bitterly and sadly.

At first his hard breathing alarmed her, and she sat waiting to avert apoplexy.

But toward morning sleep overcame her. Then daylight coming in with a shoot awakened her, and she looked round on the scene. The room in disorder, her husband sleeping off his liquor, she in her father's arm-chair, not the connubial bed.

Her first thought was, ' Oh, if father could see us now this Sabbath morn! ' She got up sadly, and lighted fires ; then went upstairs, washed and dressed the little girl, and made her lisp a prayer. Then, not choosing the daughter to see the father in his present condition, she went down and waked him, and made him wash his face and tidy himself. He asked for brandy ; she looked him in the face, and said, ' No, not one drop.' But he was ill and coaxed her. She gave him a table-spoonful, and then ground some coffee and gave him a cup hot and strong.

She was not a hasty woman ; she showed him a face grave and sad, but she did not tell him her mind. So then he opened the subject himself.

' This will be a warning to me.'

' I hope so,' said she, gravely.

'Can't think how I came to be overcome like that.'

'By putting yourself in the way of it. If you had been helping me at the shop, that needed your help, it would have been better for you, and for me too.'

'Well, I will after this. It is a warning.'

She began to relent. 'Well, James, if you take it to heart, I will not be too hard, for where is the sense of nagging at a man when he owns his fault? But, oh, James, I am so mortified! Who do you think brought you home?' He tried to remember, but could not. 'Well, one of them was the last man in Liverpool I would have to see you let yourself down so. It was Joe Pinder.'

'I never noticed him. What, was he tight too?'

'No; if he had been, I wouldn't have minded so much. He was sober, and you were——'

The man did not seize the woman's sentiment. He said, carelessly: 'Oh, 'twas he brought me safe home, was it? He is not half a bad sort, then.'

Sarah stared at this plain straightforward view of her old lover's conduct. She had a greater desire to be just than most women have, but she laboured under feminine disabilities. She was silent, and weighed Mansell's view of the matter, but came back to her own. ' I do hope,' said she, ' you will never be so overtook again—think of your child—but if you are, oh! pray don't come home on that man's arm. I'd crawl home on all fours sooner, if I was you.'

' All right,' said he, vaguely. Then she took this opportunity to beg him to go to church with her that morning. Hitherto he had always declined, but now he consented almost eagerly. He clutched at a compromise. He said, ' Sally, them that sin must suffer.' The fact is, he expected to hear his conduct denounced from the pulpit. Catch the pulpit doing anything of the kind! The pulpit is not practical, and meddles little with immorality as

it is, and rarely gives ten consecutive minutes
to that particular vice which overruns the land.
James Mansell sat under a drizzle of thin gene-
ralities, and came home complacent.

His wife was pleased with him, and still
more when he took her and Lucy for a walk in
the evening, and they carried the child by
turns.

After this the man kept within bounds; he
soaked, but could always walk home. To be
sure, he began to diffuse moderate inebriety
over the whole week. This caused the good
wife great distress of mind, and led to practical
results that alarmed the mother and the woman
of business. Mansell was still the first grainer
in the place, and the tradesmen would have
employed him by preference if he could have
been relied on to finish his jobs. But he was
so uncertain : he would go to dinner, and stop
at a public-house; would appoint an hour to
commence, and be at a public-house. He tired
out one good customer after another. The
joint income declined in consequence, and, as

generally happens, their expenses increased, for Mrs. Mansell, getting no help from her husband, was obliged to take a servant.

Often in the evening she would close her shop early, leave her child under strict charge of the girl, and go to some public-house, and there coax and remonstrate, and get him away at last.

With all this, she was as true as steel to him. She never was known to admit he was a drunkard. The most she would acknowledge to angry tradesmen, and that somewhat haughtily, was that he took a drop now and then to put away the smell of the paint.

But in private she was not so easy. She expostulated, she remonstrated, she reproached, and sometimes she lost heart, and wept bitterly at his behaviour.

All this had its effect. The invectives galled Mr. Mansell's vanity; the tears bored him; the total made him sullen, and alienated his affection. The injured party forgave freely; not so the wrong-doer. As he never hit her—

which is a vent—this gracious person began to hate her. But her love remained as invincible as his vice.

Deborah's husband died suddenly of apoplexy. Sarah dared not go to comfort her, and would not tell the reason. She begged the mourner to come to her.

Deborah came, and the sisters rocked together, country fashion, crying ; though such different characters, they had a true affection for each other.

By-and-by Deborah told her, with another burst of grief, her husband had left her nothing but debt. She was next door to a beggar.

'Not while I live,' was the quiet reply. 'Stay with me for good, that is all.' The servant was discharged at Deborah's request ; she said she must work hard or die of grief. Accordingly she went about crying, but working, and all steel things began to shine and the brass to glitter, because there was a bereaved widow in the house.

This was a great comfort in every way to

Sarah ; she could leave the house with more
confidence when her beloved had to be
dragged away from liquid ruin, and also it did
her good to sympathise with her bereaved
sister.   She forebore at that time to tell
Deborah her own trouble ; and this trait in-
dicates, I think, the depth of her character.

As for Deborah, she soon cried herself out,
and one afternoon Sarah heard her laughing
with the baker's man, laughing from the chest,
as young ladies are ordered to sing (but for-
bidden by Sir Corset), and an octave lower
than she had ever spoken upstairs since she
came.

Sarah was surprised, and almost shocked at
first.   But she said to herself, ' Poor Deb, she
is as light-hearted as ever ; and why should
she break her heart for him ? *he* wouldn't for
her.'

By-and-by Deborah used to leave the
house when her work was done, if Sarah stayed
at home.   She could not read, so she must
walk and she must talk.   She had not read a

single book this five years; but her powers of
conversation were developed. She had sold
country produce in two markets weekly, and
picked up plenty of country proverbs and
market chaff.

She soon took to visiting all her old acquaintances in the place, and talked nineteen to the
dozen; and here observe a phenomenon. Her
whole vocabulary was about nine hundred
words, whereas you and I know ten thousand
and more, yet she would ring a triple bob-major
on that small vocabulary, and talk learned us to
a standstill. As her talk was all gossip, she
soon knew more about the Mansells than they
knew themselves, and heard that Mansell drank
and lived upon his wife.

This gave her honest concern. Now she
held the clue to Sarah's absences and frequent
return with her husband in charge and inarticulate. She did not blurt it out to her sister, nor
was she angry at her want of confidence. She
knew Sarah's character, and rather admired
her for not exposing her man to any human

creature. Still, when she did know it, she threw out so many hints one after another that Sarah, who, poor soul, yearned for sympathy, made at last a partial disclosure, with many a sigh.

Deborah made light of it, and hoped it was only for a time, and after all Sarah was glad she knew, for Deborah's tongue was not in reality so loose as it was fluent. She could chatter without any appearance of reserve, and yet be as close as wax. She brought home to Sarah all she heard, but she never told anything out of the house.

One day she said to Sarah, ' Do you know a man called Varney—Dick Varney? ' Sarah said she had never heard his name.

' Then,' said Deborah, ' you ought to know him.'

' Why ?'

' Because when you know your enemy you can look out for him, and he is your enemy after a manner—for 'tis he that leads your husband astray, so that young man said.'

' What young man ? '

' I think his name is Spencer, and somebody called him Joe ; he was a good-looking chap anyway. I suppose he was a friend of Jemmy Mansell's. Somebody did praise you for a good daughter and a good wife, but one that had made a bad bargain ; then that was the signal for each to have a fling at Jemmy Mansell. Never you mind what *they* said. This handsome chap stood up for him, and said the man was a first-rate workman, and meant no harm, but he had got a tempter—this Dick Varney. So then I told the young chap who I was, and he seemed quite pleased like, and said he had heard of me. Of course what he said I stood by ; I said there couldn't be a better husband or a better man—bar drink—than James Mansell.'

Sarah thanked her, but said, ' Oh ! that we should come to be talked of ! '

' Everybody *is*, within walls,' said Deborah, ' and them that listens. learns. By the same token you keep your eye on that Varney.'

'How can I?   I don't know him.'

' No more you do, and what a stupid I must be not to ask that good-looking chap more about him.   I wonder who he is ; I will ask James.'

'No.'

'Why not?'

'Describe him to me.'

'Well, he is tall and broad-shouldered, and has light hair, and dark grey eyes like jewels, and teeth as white as milk, and a gentle, pleasant way ; looks a bit sad, he does, as if he had been crossed in love, but that is not likely—no woman would be such a fool that had eyes in her head.   Then he was very clean and neat, like a man that respected hisself ; and lowered his voice a bit to speak to a woman.   There's a duck !'

Sarah looked a little surprised at this ardent description.   However, she reflected, and, I suppose, she thought there must be some truth in it, though it had not struck her.   Then she said carelessly, ' What was his business?'

'I think he was in the same way as James himself.'

'Was his name Pinder—Joseph Pinder?'

'That, or something. The name was new to me, but Joseph for certain.'

'Well, if it is Joseph Pinder, I will ask you not to make acquaintance with *him*. You seem to be making acquaintances very fast for a woman in your condition.'

'My condition!' said Deborah. 'Why, that is where it is—I can't bear to think. I must work or talk. It is very unkind of you to cast my condition in my teeth.'

'I didn't mean to, Deb. There, forgive me.'

'With all my heart—you have got your own trouble. Only give me a reason, why am I not to speak to this Joseph—such an outlandish name—this handsome Joe?'

'Well, then, one reason is, he courted me after a fashion.'

'Oh, la! Is that where the shoe pinches?'

'We used to walk together like two children till my man came ; then they quarrelled, and that Pinder beat him, and I can't forgive it, and the first night James was quite over-taken with liquor, Pinder brought him home, and it was like a knife in my heart.'

'Poor Sally ! You saw you had chosen the wrong one.'

'Chosen the wrong one!' cried Sarah, con-temptuously. 'I wouldn't give my James's little finger, drunk or sober, for a thousand Joseph Pinders. There, it is no use talking to you. You don't understand a word I say. Anyway, I do beg of you not to make acquaint-ance with the man, nor let him know what passes in this house.'

'Why, of course not, Sally, if you say the word. What is the man to me? Your will is my pleasure, and your word my law.'

This, from an elder sister, merited an em-brace, and it received a very tender one.

At last it came to this, that nobody in the town who knew James Mansell would employ him.

Instead of contributing his share, he lived entirely on his wife, at home and abroad ; and he lived ill. So the house was divided against itself. The husband, the bread-winner in theory, was doing all he could to ruin the family ; two brave women were fighting tooth and nail to save it. They were losing ground a little, and that alarmed Sarah terribly ; but then she had a reserve : sixty pounds hidden in an iron box, with a good key. She never told her husband of this. She hid it for his good. The box was a small one, but she had it fastened with strong iron clamps to the wall, and she kept saleables before it to hide it.

Mansell's extravagance she fed from the till —not without comments, grave and sorrowful, not bitter ; yet they embittered him. The man's vanity was prodigious ; it equalled his demerit.

Whilst the brave wife and mother was thus battling with undeserved adversity, she received a new alarm.

Being single-handed in the shop, it was her way to prepare, with Deborah's assistance,

weighed and marked packets of sugar, tea, soda,
and other things; and one evening they had
taken a lump of Irish butter out of the tub and
weighed five pounds, and left it on a slab. Early
in the morning a customer came for a pound.
This was weighed off, and left so small a residue
that Mrs. Mansell weighed it, and found there
was only one pound and a half left.

She could hardly believe her senses at first,
but the weight was clear. She asked Deborah,
with assumed carelessness, how much butter they
had weighed out last night. Deborah replied,
without hesitation, ' Five pounds.'

After that day she looked more closely into
the stock, and she detected losses and diminu-
tions. One day a slice off a side of bacon; another
a tin of preserved meat; in short, a system of
pilfering. She shrank from the idea of theft, if
it could be accounted for in any other way. She
thought it just possible, though not likely, that
Deborah had made free with these things for
the use of the house. She told her what she
had discovered, and asked her as delicately as

possible whether she ever came to the shop for anything that was wanted in her kitchen.

Deborah went off like a woman of gunpowder, cross-examined by a torch : 'Me take anything out of your shop for my kitchen !'

'Well, 'tis my kitchen and all—'twould only be from Peter to Paul.'

The other was not to be pacified so. 'Me take what does not belong to me! Oh! have I lived to be suspected by my own sister? I'd cut off this arm sooner than I would steal with this hand. I never wronged a creature of a farthing or a farthing's worth in all my life. Send me home. Send me to the workhouse. I am not fit to be trusted, and so many things about. Oh! oh! oh! oh!' and down she sat and rocked.

'There! there! there!' cried Sarah, coming swiftly and sitting beside her. 'Now where would have been the harm if you had taken things for our own use? And oughtn't I to ask you before I suspected something worse? Oh, Deborah, haven't I trouble enough that you

must cry and set me off too? Oh! oh! You
might think a little of *me* as well as yourself.
Is it nothing to you that I am robbed and
all? Haven't I trouble enough without that?
There, give over—that's a dear, and I'll give
you a new print this very day.'

Deborah dried up directly, and her senti-
ments shifted like the wind. 'I wish I had
them that rob you,' said she, and she extended
her great, long, powerful arm formidably.

'We must watch day and night, dear,' said
Mrs. Mansell, gloomily, and with a weary air,
and she took it all to heart, even the pain she
had given Deborah, whose mind was like
running water, and retained no trace of the
dialogue in ten minutes. Not so the deeper
nature. Mrs. Mansell brooded over it all, and
when the shop was shut, she sat in the parlour
—sat and suffered. James Mansell was out as
usual. She sat and looked at Lucy, and
wondered what would be her own fate and her
child's at the end of this desperate struggle.
She became hysterical, a rare thing with her,

and Deborah found her trembling all over where she sat, and quite shaken. She was despondent and exasperated by turns. She had twitches all over her body, and hot tears ran out of her eyes.

It was a woman's breakdown, and Deborah, who knew the female constitution, just sat beside her and held her hand. Sarah clung to this hand, and clutched it every now and then convulsively. She spoke in broken sentences. ' Too many things against me: drunkenness here ; theft there. It will end in the workhouse! How else can it end? I'm glad father's dead. Poor father !—have I lived to say that ? ' The talkative Deborah said never a word, so Sarah began to calm down by degrees with gentle sighs and tremors.

Unluckily, before she was quite calm, Mansell knocked at the door. Sarah could tell his knock, or his footstep, or any sound he made in a moment. Her face beamed. It was early for him. He was sober, and she could tell him of this new trouble.

Deborah ran to let him in. Sarah stood up smiling to welcome him.

He blundered into the room, beastly drunk, neckcloth loose, eyes blood-shot; he could just keep on his legs.

Sarah caught up her child with the strength of a lioness, flung one full and fiery look of horror and disgust right in her husband's face, then rushed majestically from the room, carrying her child across her arms.

Drunk as he was, the brute staggered under this tremendous glance and eloquent rush. He blundered against the mantel-piece, and hung his head.

Deborah set her arms akimbo: 'You've done this once too often,' she said, grimly, and her eyes glittered at him wickedly.

'Mind your own business,' said he. 'Why did she run away from me like that?'

'Because of the child, you may be sure. There, don't let us quarrel. Will you have your supper, now you are here?'

'I don't want my supper; I want my wife.

You go and fetch her directly.' He was excited, and Deborah, determined to keep the
peace, took his message to Sarah in Lucy's
bedroom.

Sarah was shaking all over, and refused to
come. 'I dare not,' said she. 'I am in such
a state I feel I might say or do something I
should rue afterward, for I love him. Would
to God I had never seen him, but I love him.
Go you and pacify him. I shall sleep here
beside my child.'

Deborah went down, and found Mansell in
the arm-chair, looking spiteful. She told him
Sarah was not well. She could not come down.

'Humbug!' roared James Mansell; 'she is
shamming. I'll go and fetch her down,' and
he bounced up. Deborah whipped before the
door. 'Stand out of my way,' said he, loftily,
and came blundering at her. She pinned him
directly by the collar with both hands, shook
him to and fro as a dog does a rat, then put
both hands suddenly to his breast, made a
grand rush forward with him, and with the

double power of her loins and her great long
arms, shot him all across the room into the
arm-chair with such an impetus that the chair
went crashing against the wall, and the man in
it head down, feet up.

Mr. Mansell stared dumbfoundered at first.
He thought some supernatural power had disposed of him. He did not allow for sudden-
ness, and was not aware that pulling and
pushing go by weight, and that strapping
Deborah, without an ounce of fat, weighed two
stone more than he did, owing to certain laws
of construction not worth particularising *à la
française.*

' I never lay my hand on a woman,' said
he, moodily.

' I'm not so nice,' replied Deborah, erect,
with her fists upon her hips. ' I can lay my
hands on a man—for his good. I've had that
much to do afore now, and I never found one
could master me, bar hitting, which I call that
cowardly.'

Then, as time was up for a change of sentiment—eighty whole seconds—she shifted to friendly advice.

'Jemmy, my man,' said she, 'women are curious creatures. They are not themselves at times. Our Sally has got the nerves. She might fling a knife at you if you tormented her just now, sobbing over her child. Take my advice, now, that is a friend to both of you. Let her a-be. If you don't upset her no more to-night, which I declare *you sha'n't,* she'll be as sweet as honey in the morning.'

'She may,' said Mansell, sullenly, 'but I shall not. If she lies away from me to-night, I'll lie away from her a year or more, mind that.'

'Where? In the union?'

'No. That is as much as to say she keeps me.'

'And doesn't she? Where does the money come from you spend in drink?'

'I have got an offer of work.'

'Work? It isn't under your skin.'

'Not here, but this is in America. Such work as mine is paid out there, and I can make my fortune, and not have it flung in my face I'm living on a woman.'

Deborah did not think this gasconade worth replying to. She suggested repose as the best thing for him after the hard work he had gone through, lifting mugs and quarterns all the way from the counter to his teeth. With much trouble she got him up the stairs, and took off his neckcloth and loosened his shirt collar. Then she retired for a reasonable time, and when he was in bed came and took away the candle from him as she would from a child. He called to her :

'Hear my last word.'

'No such luck,' said she, drily.

'Hold your tongue.'

'If I hold my tongue I shall slobber my teeth.'

'Can you listen a moment ? '

'If I hold my breath.'

'Then mind this. If she leaves me like this, I'll leave *her*. I won't be taken up and put down by any woman.'

'I'll tell her, my man,' said she, to quiet him; then took away his candle, and went downstairs to her own room, for she slept on the kitchen floor. She seized a feather-bed, lugged it up the stairs, and made up a bed on the floor for Sarah. 'He is all right,' said she, and not a word more. Then she went downstairs, and put her red hair in curl-papers—for she was flirting all round, No. 1 had been dead six months—and slept like a stone upon a hard mattress, not harder than her own healthy limbs.

CHAPTER III.

WHAT wonderful restoratives are a good long sleep and the dawn of day! They co-operate so, invigorating the body and fortifying the mind. They clear away the pain and the forebodings night engenders, and brighten not only the face of nature, but our individual prospects. The glorious dawn falling upon our refreshed eyes and invigorated bodies is like a trumpet sounding 'Nil desperandum!' Mrs. Mansell was one of the many whom sleep and dawn reinspired and reconciled to her lot that morning. She had slept in a pure atmosphere—untarnished by a drunkard's breath. She awoke with her nerves composed and her heart strengthened.

Her life was to be a battle—that was plain. But she had forces and an ally. Her forces were rare health, strength, prudence, and sobriety. Her ally was Deborah. She began the battle this morning brightly and hopefully. She was the first up, and having dressed herself neatly, as she always did, she put on a large apron and bib, coarse but clean, and descended to the parlour. She called up the spiral staircase—'James!'

No answer.

She went into the shop, and called down the kitchen stairs. No reply from her sister. 'Lazy-bones,' said she. She struck a light in the shop, and her eye fell upon a large handbell. She took it up and rang it down the kitchen stairs. Instantly there was a sort of yawn of distress. Then she bustled into the parlour, and rang it up the spiral staircase. Then she set it down, and took her candle into the shop, and sorted, and dusted, and counted the goods, and cleaned the counter.

Presently in sauntered Deborah from the kitchen, with her hair in curl-papers, and a chasm in the upper part of her gown, so that

she seemed half-dislocated ; and she adhered
to the wall for support, and sprawled out one
long arm and a hand, which she flattened
against the wall, to hold on by suction sooner
than not at all. 'Here's a [yawn] to-do,' said
she. 'Anybody's [yawn] cat dead?'

'No, but mine are catching no mice. Nobody to light the fire and give my man his
breakfast while I open the shop. Aren't you
ashamed of yourself?'

'Too sleepy [yawn] to be ashamed of anything !'

'Then wake up and bustle.'

Deborah gave herself a wriggle that set
her long bare arms flying like windmills, and
went to work. The pair soon brightened the
parlour, and then Sarah came into the shop and
opened the door ; but the patent shutters outside were heavy and stiff, as she knew, so she
called Deborah.

'You might pull down those heavy shutters
outside for me. You are stronger than I am,
for all you look like a jelly-bag.'

Deborah drew back in dismay. 'Me go into the street! I'm not half dressed.'

'Fine shapes don't need fine clothes. You might catch another husband on the pavement.'

'I'd rather catch him in church with my new bonnet.' Then, to escape any more invitations to publish her curl-papers—for that was where the shoe really pinched—she ran maliciously into the parlour, screaming up the corkscrew stairs: 'Here, master! James Mansell, you are wanted!'

'Be quiet,' said Sarah, colouring; 'he is not your servant. Them that do it for me will be round directly. It isn't the master's business to take down the wife's shutters.'

'I think it is, then, if he is a man, for it is a man's work.'

Deborah spoke this at James Mansell, and at the top of her voice. The words were hardly out of her mouth when a man's hands were seen to pull down the heavy shutters and let in the light.

E

'Didn't I tell you?' said the ready Deborah. 'And here is one dropped from the sky express.'

'Why, it is Joseph Pinder,' said Mrs. Mansell, drawing back.

'La! Your old sweetheart!'

'Never! For shame! Hold your tongue!'

Deborah grinned with delight, and whipped into the parlour to hide her curl-papers and listen. Sarah went behind the counter and minded her business. She made sure Pinder would proceed on his course, as soon as he had done that act of courtesy.

Instead of that he came slowly and a little sheepishly in at the door, and stood at the counter opposite her. He was in a complete suit of white cotton, all but his soft brown hat, and looked wonderfully neat and clean.

'Good-morning, Mrs. Mansell,' said he, respectfully.

'Good-morning, Mr. Pinder,' said Mrs. Mansell. Then—stiffly—'Sorry you should take so much trouble.'

Pinder looked puzzled, so, woman-like, she answered his looks.

'I mean to take down my shutters. I pay a person express.'

'Oh, I heard somebody say it was a man's work.'

Sarah explained hurriedly : 'Oh, that was my sister.'

'What, Deborah?'

'Deborah,' said she, drily, in a way calculated to close the dialogue. But Pinder did not move. He fumbled with his hat, and at last said he was not there by accident, but had come to see her.

'What for?' And she opened her eyes rather wide.

'A little bit of business.'

Sarah coloured, but she said drily, 'What can I serve you?'

'Oh, it is not with *you*; it is with your husband.'

'Indeed,' said she, rather incredulously, almost suspiciously.

'Got him a job.'

'That is very good of you, I'm sure,' was the reply, and now the tone was satirical. 'My husband has plenty of jobs.'

'Well, he used to have; but the shop-keepers here are against him now; they say he leaves his work.'

Sarah seized this opportunity to get rid of Mr. Pinder altogether. 'Did you come here to run my husband down to me?' she inquired, haughtily.

'Am I one of that sort?' said Pinder, defiantly. He was beginning to take offence, as well he might. 'I came to do the man a good turn, whether I get any thanks for it or not.'

Sarah coloured and held her peace. He had taken the right way with her now. But it was hard for the good-natured fellow to hold spite, especially against her; he went naturally back to his friendly manner, and told her that the new Rectory was being decorated by a London firm, and their grainer had been taken

ill, and he (Pinder) had told the foreman he
knew a tiptop grainer, James Mansell, and the
foreman had jumped at him.

'I've made the bargain, Sarah. London
price. It's a thirty-pound job.' And he
looked proud.

' Thirty pounds?' exclaimed Sarah.

' Yes; it's a large house, panelled rooms,
and hall and staircase, all to be grained, besides
the doors and shutters, and skirtings. Only
mind, these swell London tradesmen won't
stand—unpunctuality. Where is he, if you
please?'

' Oh, he is at home.'

' Then let me see him directly.'

' You can't just now.'

Deborah, who had listened to every word,
chose this moment to emerge from the parlour.
She had utilised her curl-papers by lighting the
fire with them, and came out very neat in a
charming cap, and curtsied. 'Give him
half an hour, Mr. Pinder,' said she, sweetly;
' he is in bed.'

Pinder looked at his watch, and said he
could not wait half an hour—he was due; but
he wrote a line with his pencil for Mansell
to give to the foreman; then he put on
his cap and said, jauntily, 'Good-morning,
ladies.'

'Good morning, sir,' said Deborah, gra-
ciously.

'And thank you, Joseph,' said Sarah,
gently.

'You are very welcome; I suppose you
know that,' said he, as bluntly as he could.

When he was gone, Sarah's artificial indifference disappeared with a vengeance. She ran
into the parlour, and screamed up the spiral
staircase, 'James! James! Such good news!
Get up and come down directly!'

'All right,' said a sleepy voice.

Then she turned on Deborah. 'And what
call had you to say he was in bed?'

'Oh, the truth may be blamed, but it can't
be shamed,' was Deborah's steady reply.

. Proverbs being unanswerable, Sarah changed

the subject. 'And if you haven't got on my new cap!'

Deborah had no by-word ready to justify misappropriation of another lady's cap; so she took a humble tone. ' La! Sally, I couldn't help it, he was such a nice young man. You can't abide him, but tastes they differ. Do you think he will come again? If he does, I really must set my cap at him.'

'But not *mine*;' and Sarah, who was in rare spirits, whipped her cap in a moment off her sister's head.

'La! you needn't to take my hair and all,' whined Deborah. 'That's my own, anyway.'

'Then you are not in the fashion,' was the ready reply. 'Come, Deb, enough chat; this is a busy morning, and a happy morning to make us forget last night for ever. Now, dear, run and make my man his coffee—nice and strong.'

'I will.'

'And clean his boots for going out.'

'If I must, I must,' said Deborah, with

sudden languor. She never could see why
women should clean men's boots.

'And air him a shirt.'

'Is that all?' inquired Deborah, affecting
surprise.

'All at present,' said the mistress, drily.

'What, hasn't he any hose to darn, nor hair
to be cut, nor teeth to be cleaned for him?'

'You go on, with your cheek,' and she
threatened Deborah merrily with a duster. Her
heart was light. And now a customer or two
trickled in at intervals. She served them
promptly and civilly.

Presently she saw her husband coming
slowly down the spiral staircase. She ran into
the parlour to meet him. Not a word about
last night, but welcomed him with smiles
and a long kiss. 'Good news, dear,' said she,
jubilant.

He received her with discouraging languor :
'Well, what is up?'

But she was not to be disheartened so
easily. 'Why, Jemmy dear! there's a job

waiting for you at the Rectory, and you are
to have thirty pounds for it.'

'Thirty pounds!   That will be a long job.'

She tossed her head a little at that.   'Why
a long job?   It is not day-work.   It shouldn't
be a long job if I had it to do, and was as
clever as you are.   Come, here's Deborah with
your coffee and nice hot toast.   Eat your
breakfast and start.   No, don't take it into the
parlour, Deb, to waste more time; set it down
here on the flap.   I do love to see him eat.'

Mr. Mansell, thus stimulated, put the coffee
to his lips.   But he set it down untasted, and
said he couldn't.

'Try, dear; 'twill do you good.'

'I can't, Sally; I am very ill; my head
swims so, and my chest is on fire.   Oh!' and
Mr. Mansell leaned on the end of the counter
and groaned aloud.   He made so much of his
disease that Sarah was alarmed, and told
Deborah to run for the doctor.

That personage stood stock-still, and
as ostentatiously calm as the invalid was

demonstrative in his sufferings. 'A doctor! Why, he'd make the man ill.' She folded her arms and contemplated the victim. 'Hot coppers,' said she. 'He only wants a hair of the dog that bit him.' This with a composure that befitted the occasion; but it was not so received. 'How dare you!' cried Sarah.

'Yes, Deb, for mercy's sake,' moaned the sufferer—'for mercy's sake, a drop of brandy!'

Deborah would have gone for it directly if she had been mistress, but, as it was, she consulted her sister by the eye.

Sarah replied to that look with great decision. 'Not if you are any sister of mine. Ay, that is the way of it—drink to be ill, and then drink to be well; and once you have begun, go on till you are ill again, and want a drop to start you again on the road to beggary and shame. Drink, drink, drink! in a merry-go-round that never halts.' Then, firmly: '*You* drink *your* coffee without more words, and then go and work for your daughter like a man. Come!'

She held the cup out to him with a fine air
of authority, though her heart was quaking all
the time, and he, being just then in a subdued
condition, took it resignedly, and sipped a little.
Then a customer came in, but Sarah was not
to be diverted from her purpose. She ordered
Deborah to stand there and see him drain every
drop. Deborah folded her bare arms and
inspected the process loftily but keenly. He got
through two-thirds of the contents, then showed
her the balance with such a piteous look that
she had compassion, stretched out her long arm
for the cup, sent the contents down her throat
with one gesture, and returned the cup with
another gesture, half regal, half vulgar, all in
two seconds, and James with admirable rapidity
set the cup down empty under Sarah's eye, and
so they abused her confidence.

'Well done,' said she ; 'strong coffee is an
antidote, they say, and work is another. Off
you go to the Rectory, and work till one.
Deborah will have a nice hot dinner ready for
you by then.' She found him his basket and

his brushes, all cleaned by herself, though he had left them foul.

At this last trait a gleam of gratitude shot into his skull. He said: 'Well, you are the right sort. It is some pleasure to work for you.'

'And our child,' said she. 'Think of us both when you think of one. Oh, Jemmy dear! if you should ever be tempted again, do but ask yourself whether them that tempt you to your ruin love you as well as we do.'

'Say no more, Sally; I'll turn a new leaf. Here, give me a kiss over the counter.' So they had a long conjugal embrace over the counter.

Deborah looked on, and said, in her way, 'Makes my mouth water, being a widder.'

'There,' said James Mansell, turning to go. 'I'll never touch a drop again until I have chucked that thirty pounds into your lap, my girl.' With this resolve, he left the shop.

Sarah must come round the corner, and watch him down the street; then she turned at the door, and beamed all over, and her eyes sparkled. 'God bless him!' she cried. 'There isn't a better workman, nor a better husband, nor a better man, in Britain, only keep him from drink. Now is there?'

'La! Sarah, how can I tell? I never saw him sober six days running; but I have heard you say he used to be a good husband. And why not again, if he do but keep his word?'

'And he will; he is not the man to break his word, far less his oath. He turns over a new leaf to-day, and I'm a happy woman once more.'

'And I'll have his dinner ready to the moment.'

Deborah dived into the kitchen, and was heard the next moment working and whistling tunes of a cheerful character. No blacksmith or ploughboy could beat this rustic dame at that.

Mrs. Mansell was soon occupied at the counter. A cook came in, and bought three pounds of bacon at 8d. the pound for her

mistress, and ditto of best Limerick at 11*d.* for
the kitchen—these prices to be reversed in her
housekeeping book. She also paid the week's
bill, and demanded her perquisite. Sarah sub-
mitted, and gave her half a crown, or her mistress would have shopped elsewhere under her
influence. Then came a maid-of-all-work for a
packet of blacklead, seven pounds of soda, two
of sugar, a bar of soap, and some ' connubial '
blacking. Sarah said she was out of that. The
slavey replied, with the usual attention to
grammar: ' Oh yes, you do! Mrs. White's
servant buys it here.'

' Oh, that's Nubian blacking.'

' Well, and that's what I want; saves a vast
o' trouble.'

Others came, child customers, some only
just up to the counter, and many of them mute.
These showed their coppers, and Sarah had to
divine the rest. But she had a rare eye for
them; she looked keenly at each mite, and
knew what they wanted by their faces and
their coin. She gave one a screw of tobacco

for father, another a candle with paper wrapped round the middle, another an ounce of candy. But as it drew near one there was a lull in trade, and savoury smells came up from the kitchen. The good wife must have a finger in her husband's dinner. She locked the shop door and ran down to the kitchen fire, and when it had struck one, and everything was done to a turn, she ran up again and unlocked the door and laid a clean cloth in the little parlour, and had Lucy there very neat, that no attraction might be wanting to her converted husband and workman on his return to his well-earned meal.

By-and-by Deborah looked in with cheeks as red as her hair to say the steak would spoil if not eaten.

'But you mustn't *let* it spoil,' objected Sarah, loftily. 'He won't be long now'—then, with delight—'here he is,' for a man's figure darkened the door. 'No; it's only Joseph Pinder.'

Joseph Pinder it was, and for once looking morose. He had a tin can with a narrowish neck in his hand, and put it down on the counter with some noise, as much as to say, 'This time I am a customer and nothing more.' Mrs. Mansell received him as such, went behind the counter directly, and leaned a little over, awaiting his orders.

'Half a gallon of turps,' said he, almost rudely. Mrs. Mansell went meekly and filled his can from a little tank with a tap.

But Deborah, who never read books, always read faces. She scanned Pinder, and said, 'You seem put out. Is there anything the matter?'

'Plenty,' said he; 'more than I like to tell. But she must know it sooner or later. Serves me right, anyway, for recommending a——'

He stopped in time, and turned away from Sarah to Deborah, and said bitterly, 'He never came to work at all. He fell in with a tempter in this very street, and got enticed away directly.'

Sarah raised her hands in dismay, and uttered not a word, but an inarticulate cry of

distress, so eloquent of amazement and dismay
that Pinder's anger gave way to pity, and he
began all of a sudden to make excuses for the
offender, and lay the blame on Dick Varney, a
dangerous villain with a cajoling tongue, a
pickpocket's fingers, and a heart of stone. He
turned to Sarah now, and enlarged on this
villain's vices—said he had been in prison
twice, and it was he who was ruining James
Mansell.

But Sarah interrupted all this: ' Never
mind him. Where is my poor husband ? '

' At " The Chequers," my mate says.'

' Give me my shawl and bonnet, Deborah.'

' What to do ? ' inquired Pinder, uneasily.

' To fetch him away,' was the dogged
reply.

Then at last the long-hidden truth came out.
' Oh, it will not be the first time I have gone to
a public-house, and stood their jeers and his
drunken anger for an hour or two, and brought
him home at last. He has sworn at me before
them all, but he never struck me. Perhaps

F

that is to come. I think it will come to-day,
for he was more violent last night than ever I
knew him to be. I don't care, I'll have him
home if I die for it.'

'Not from "The Chequers," you won't.
You don't know the place ; there are bad women
there as well as bad men. Why, it's a boozing-
ken for thieves and their jades. Take a man
away from them !—they would soil your ears
and make your flesh creep, and perhaps mark
your face for ever. You stay beside your
sister. I must go on with it now. I'll strike
work at dinner-time for once in my life, and I'll
bring your man home.'

This melted both the sisters, Sarah most,
who had been so cold to her old lover. 'Oh,
thank you, bless you, Joseph !' she sobbed.

'Don't cry, Sally,' said the honest fellow, in
a broken voice ; 'pray don't cry ! I can't bear
to see you cry,' and he almost burst out of the
place for fear he should break down himself, or
say something kinder than he ought. His boy
was waiting outside ; he sent him in for the

turps, and ordered him to tell the foreman to dock his afternoon time, he was gone to look after the grainer.

He went down to ' The Chequers,' and got there just in time to find Mansell quarrelling with three blackguards in the skittle-ground. Indeed, before he could interfere, one of them gave the drunken man a severe blow on the nose that made him bleed like a pig. The next moment the aggressor lay flat on his back, felled by Joe Pinder. The other two sparred up, but went down like nine-pins before that long, muscular arm, shot out straight from the shoulder. Then he seized Mansell, and said, ' The villains have hurt you ; come and be cured.' And so, not giving him time to think, he half coaxed, half pushed him out of the place, and got him on the road home.

Meantime Sarah sat sorrowful, and said her happy day was soon ended, and she wished her life was ended too. Deborah sat beside her, and tried to comfort her.

' One good thing,' said she, ' you have got

a friend now, when most wanted, and "a friend in need is a friend indeed." And to think you had the offer of Joseph Pinder, and could go and take James Mansell!'

Sarah drew up: 'And would again,' said she, 'with all his faults. I would not give him for Joe Pinder, nor any other man.'

'Well, that's a good job, as you are tied to him,' remarked Deborah.

'Do you think Joseph will bring him home?'

'If any man can. I think ever so much of that chap.'

'Then don't let the dinner spoil, at all events.'

Deborah didn't trust herself to speak. She got up resignedly to attend to the possible wants of this deserving husband. Sarah divined that it cost her a struggle, and tried to gild the pill.

'You are a good sister to me,' said she.

'That I am,' said Deborah, frankly. 'But so are you to me; and I was always as fond of you as a cow is of her calf.'

'And I haven't forgot the print,' said Mrs. Mansell; 'but you see how I have been put about. I mustn't go to my safe even for you, but there's half a sovereign in the till, and you shall have it before some fresh trouble comes to make me forget.'

Deborah's eyes sparkled, but she said it wasn't a fit time, there were too many sucking at her.

'And that is true; but they can't drain me. Don't tell a soul; I make a deal of money in this little shop. I wouldn't give my Saturdays for 5*l.* apiece.' Then almost in a whisper : 'I've got 60*l.* put by in that safe there, and the safe fastened to the wall. I mustn't touch that money, 'tis for my darling Lucy. But there's an odd half-sovereign in the till, and it is for you. There are some beauties at Coverley's, over the way.' Dress, having once been mentioned, was, of course, the dominant substantive. Whilst she was speaking, she took out her keys and opened the till. There was much less silver in it than she expected to find. She put both hands in, and turned it all over in a moment. There was no half-sovereign. 'Come here! come here!' she screamed; 'the till has been robbed.'

'La, Sarah,' cried Deborah, 'never!'

'But I say it has; there's not a shilling here but what I have taken to day.'

'When did you look last?'

'Yestereen at six, and counted half a sovereign and eighteen shillings in silver. What will become of me now?—there are thieves about. Heaven knows how the goods go, but this is some man's work.'

'Then I wish I had him,' said Deborah, and she thrust out her great arms and long, sinewy fingers. The words were scarcely out of her lips, and the formidable fingers still extended, knuckles downward, when James Mansell, his shirt and trousers covered with blood, was thrust in at the door by Joseph Pinder: his own white dress had suffered by the contact.

Both women screamed at sight of him,

and Sarah cried, 'Oh! they have murdered him.'

Pinder said, hastily, ' No, no, he's none the worse—only a bloody nose.'

' Then he is cheap served,' said Deborah.

'Ay, but let me tell you I came just in time : there were three of them on to him.'

' Oh,' cried Sarah, ' the cowards ! '

Mr. Mansell caught at the word ' cowards.' Cried he, ' Let's go and fight 'em.'

' Not if I know it,' said Pinder, stopping his rush, and holding him like a vice.

' What, are you turned coward and all ? Look here, he knocked 'em all three down like nine-pins.'

' Then there let 'em lie,' said this rational hero.

' I sha'n't,' said the irrational one. ' I'll go and just kick 'em up again, and then——'

But the next process was not revealed, because in illustrating the first Mr. Mansell sat down on the floor with a heavy bump, and had to be picked up by Pinder and lectured.

' What you want just now is not more fighting, but a wash, and then a sleep.'

Sarah proposed an amendment : ' What he wants most, Mr. Pinder, is a heart and a conscience.'

' Is that all ? ' said the impenitent.

Deborah giggled. But Mr. Mansell had better have kept his humour for a less serious situation. The much-enduring wife turned upon him the moment he spoke :

' After all you promised and swore to me this day.   Good work and good money brought to your hand by one we had no claim on, either you or I, a good home to come to, a good dinner cooked with loving hands, and a good wife and daughter that counted the minutes till they could see you eating it.   What are you made of?   You are neither a husband, nor a father, nor a man.'

CHAPTER IV.

'Hold your tongue!' roared the culprit.

But her blood was fairly up, and instead of flinching from him, she came at him like a lioness.

'No : I have held my tongue long enough and screened your faults, and hid my trouble from the world. What right have such men as you to marry and get children that they hate and would beggar if they could, as well as their miserable wives?' She put her hand suddenly to her forehead as a keen pain shot through it. 'He will drive me wild. If you are a sister of mine, take him out of my sight.' She stamped her foot on the ground, and her eyes flashed : 'D'ye hear? Take him out of my sight before my heart bursts my bosom, and I curse the hour I ever saw him.'

Deborah had bundled him into the parlour before this climax came, and she now got him out of sight altogether, saying, 'Come, Jemmy! "A wise man never faces an angry woman."'

As for Sarah, she sank down upon a seat, languid and limp; and after the thunder the rain.

Pinder, with instinctive good-breeding, had turned to go. But now he couldn't. The woman he had always loved, and who had given him so much pain, sat quietly weeping, as one who could no longer struggle. He looked at her, and, to use the expressive words of Scripture, his bowels yearned over her. He did not know what he could say to do her any good, yet he couldn't go without trying. He said, gently, 'Don't despair; while there's life there's hope.'

She shook her head sadly, and said, gently, 'There's none for me now.'

'Oh, yes; if that Varney could be got out of the way, *he* would listen to reason. He is the wicked one; your man is only weak.'

'Where's the odds if they do the same thing? But it is very good of you to make excuses for him.'

She then took out a white pocket-handkerchief and meekly dried her eyes; then she stood up and said, in a grave, thoughtful way —which he recognised as her old manner— 'Let me look at you.'

She took a step toward him, but he did not move toward her. On the contrary, he stood there and fidgeted, and when she looked full at him he hung down his head a little.

'Nay, look at me,' said she; 'you have done naught to be ashamed of.'

Being so challenged, he did look at her, but not so full as she did at him. It was a peculiarity of this woman that she could gaze into a man's face without either seeming bold or feeling ashamed. She never took her eye off Pinder's face during the whole dialogue which follows. Said she, slowly and thoughtfully, and her eye perusing him all the time: 'You must be a very good young man. Years

ago you courted me honourably, and I was
barely civil to you.'

Pinder said, gently, 'You never deceived
me.'

. 'No, but I never valued you. Now that
I am older, I have noticed that for a woman
to refuse a man makes him as bitter as gall.
Dear heart! do but wound his vanity, and his
love, such as 'tis, turns to spite directly; but
instead of that you have always spoken re-
spectful of me, for it has come round to my
ears; and you have held aloof from me, and
that was wise and proper, till you saw I was
in trouble, and then you came to me to do me
a good turn in the right way through my
unfortunate husband. You are one of a thousand, and may God reward you!'

By this time Pinder's eyes had gradually
sunk to the ground before the calm gaze and
the intelligent praise of one who was still very
dear to him.

'Have you done?' said he, drily, inspect-
ing the floor.

' Yes,' said she ; ' I have thought my thought and said my say.'

' Well, then, I should like to tell you something.   It makes a man better to love a good woman, even if he can't win her and wear her. I studied you when you were a maid, and it set me against a many vulgar vices.   I have had my eye on you since you were a wife, and that has made me respect you still more, and respect virtue.   You have a dangerous enemy in that Dick Varney.   Against him you want a friend. I seem to feel somehow as if I was called upon to be that friend, and I do assure you, Sarah, that I am not so unreasonable as I was when the disappointment was fresh.   I should have been downright happy to-day if things had gone to your mind.   After all, the day isn't over yet, and I've struck work.   Is there nothing I can do Drink and Dick Varney can't spoil, confound them ? '

Thus urged, and being beset with troubles, and feeling already the rare comfort and support of a male friend, she confessed she had another trouble—a small one comparatively, but not a small one on the top of the others. She was being robbed. She told him all about it, and with a workman's quickness he asked to see the lock of the till.

He examined this closely, and detected at once, by abrasions in the metal, that it had been opened with a picklock, not a key. He told her so, and she said she was none the wiser.

'I am, though,' said he. 'It shows that nobody in the house has done it. It's professional. I should not wonder if this was Varney and all. Why, he's an old hand at this game, and has been in trouble for no other thing. Does he ever come into your shop?'

'He may. I don't know him by sight.'

Pinder reflected. 'James Mansell tells him everything, you may be sure, and it's just like the scoundrel to steal in here and rob the wife at home, and ruin the husband abroad.'

Then he thought again, and presently

slapped his thigh with satisfaction, for he thought he saw a way to turn all this to profit.

'If we can only catch that Varney, and give him five years' penal—it won't be less, being an old offender—Mansell will lose his tempter, and then he'll listen to you and me, strike drink, go in for work, and be a much happier man, and you a happy woman.'

'Oh, these are comforting words!' said poor Sarah. 'But how am I to catch the villain?'

'Others must do that. You go to the police station, see the Superintendent, and make your complaint. I'll come after you, and talk to Mr. Steele, the detective; he is a friend of mine, and will soon know all about it. A drunken thief is as leaky as the rest. But you must keep your own counsel; your sister has a good heart, but she is a chatterbox, and out every evening in half a dozen houses. I don't like to go with you because of the blood on my clothes; but if you will start at

once, I will change my coat and join you at
the station, and bring you back.'

Sarah carried out these instructions with
her usual fidelity. She ascertained that her husband was lying fast asleep upon the bed; she
put on her shawl and bonnet, confided Lucy
and the shop to Deborah, and when the latter
asked where she was going, said, drily, 'There
and back.' With that she vanished.

'There, now,' said Deborah, 'I owe that to
you, Mr. Pinder.'

'How so?'

'When they have got a nice young man to
tell their minds to, they don't waste words on a
sister.'

'Well, you needn't grudge me,' said he.
'It's five years since she spoke a word to me.'
So then he retired in his turn, and Deborah
had only the customers and little Lucy to talk
to.

The customers of this little shop, accustomed
to the grave, modest Sarah, must have been a
little surprised at the humours of her substitute.

The first to be astonished was a game-keeper. He came in, spruce in velveteen jacket and leathern gaiters, from the country. He stared at Deborah, none the less that she happened just then to be whistling a poacher's song.

'Why, where's the mistress?' said he.

'Gone after the master.'

'And where's the master?'

'Gone before the mistress.'

'I want a pound o' powder.'

'Well, money will buy it. What powder? Emery-powder, putty-powder, violet-powder?'

'No, gunpowder, to be sure.'

Deborah recoiled : 'I wouldn't touch it for a pension.'

The gamekeeper laughed. 'Well,' said he, ' you are a pretty shopwoman.'

'Oh, sir,' said Deborah, coquettishly, 'and I'm sure you are a beautiful gamekeeper.'

He took a considerable time to comprehend this retort ; when he had mastered the diffi-culty, he said, ' Well, let us trade. You'll beat me at talk. Powder isn't loose; it's in a canister.'

'Oh,' said Deborah, 'you seem to know all about it. Where does she keep it?'

'Why, there 'tis, right under your nose.'

'Well, I can't see with my nose, can I?'

She took it and put it rather gingerly on the counter. 'Now before it goes off and sends us all to Heaven or Somewhere, what is the price of it, if you please.'

'Oh, the seller sets the price,' said he.

'All right,' said she. 'Ten shillings! See what a lot you can kill with it.'

'The mistress always makes it half a crown.'

'Ay,' said Deborah, 'she is a hard woman. You give me a shilling, and I'll only charge you eighteenpence.'

While he was counting out the money, a keen whistle was heard. Deborah's quick ears caught it directly: 'Is that for you?' said she.

'No; more likely for you.'

' All the better. " Whistle and I'll come to you, my lad," ' said she, directing the invitation out into the street.

' I'd step out and whistle if I thought that,' said the gamekeeper, showing his whistle. ' Shall I try? '

' Why not?

It's a man's part to try,
And a woman's to deny,
And now you'd better fly,

for here comes our family sponge. Well, he does shake off liquor quick, I must say that for him.'

James Mansell came through the parlour, clean washed and very neatly dressed.

' Mrs. Smart,' said he, civilly.

' Mr. Mansell, I hope I see you well, sir. It's you for quick recoveries. Bloody noses is good for the brain, apparently,' suggested Deborah, ' likewise a little repose after the fatigue of drinking and fighting.

' I did take forty winks.'

' Well, sir, and now you are fortified, what's

the next order? Another cup of coffee, war-
ranted to contain a little chicory, and a deal of
bullock's liver, acorns, burned rags, and
muck?'

'No; after this last experience I've for-
sworn all liquids except juicy meat and rotten
potatoes. And I should feel greatly obliged if
you would prepare me a nice hot steak, and fry
me some onions nice and brown, as you alone
can fry them.'

'It is the least any woman can do for such a
civil-spoken gentleman,' said Deborah, and she
dived at once into her kitchen, telling him to
mind the shop. She little thought that his
great object was to get rid of her.

He watched her out, and then went to the
shop-door and looked out. It was Varney's
whistle that had drawn him, and that worthy
was waiting, and upon Mansell's invitation came
cautiously in. Never was thief more plainly
marked on a human being. His little, lank,
wriggling body reminded one of a weasel, and
his eyebrows seemed to spring from his temples

and meet on the bridge of his nose. The eyes thus framed could not keep still a moment. They were like a hare's ears, in constant alarm. Between this man and Mansell an eager dialogue took place, rapid and low, which nobody heard but themselves. But anyone who saw the speakers would feel sure those two were plotting some vile thing.

Something or other was definitely settled, even in that short time, and then Varney, who was ill at ease in that place, invited Mansell to turn out at once.

Mansell objected that he was famished, and dinner was being prepared.

'No, no,' said the other; 'I won't stay here. You follow me to Buck's dining-room; and mind, no more liquor for me to-day. It will be a ticklish job.'

He wriggled away, and Mansell took his hat, and called down the kitchen stairs : 'Mrs. Smart—Deborah—please come up here, and attend to the shop. I'm wanted for a job.'

Deborah raised no objection, but she

resolved on the spot that the steak she had twice prepared for a fool should now be eaten by a rational being, and to make quite sure of this she would eat it herself. So she put a little cloth on a tray, with the steak and two potatoes, and ran up with it all, and put this savoury supper on the flap, and had just made her first incision, when in came one of the little mites I have referred to, intelligible to Sarah alone. The mite rapped the counter with a penny. Deborah left her steak and faced him :

'What can I serve you, sir?'

The mite hammered the counter with his copper.

'Oh, yes,' said Deborah, 'I see what I am to have out of you; but what are you to have for all that money?' Then she leaned over the child : 'Is it baccy? Is it soap? It should be soap if I was your mother, you little pig. You won't tell me, eh? It's a dead secret. Let's try another way!' And she put down the likeliest articles one after another. 'There,

a penn'orth o' baccy for father ; a penn'orth o'
soap ; a penn'orth o' lollipops.' The child
grabbed the lollipops in a moment and left the
copper, and Deborah dashed back to her steak,
muttering, ' Sally would have known what he
wanted by the colour of his hair.'

There was a run on the shop. For every
three mouthfuls of steak, a penny customer.
Deborah despatched them how she could, then
dashed back to her steak—in vain : it was an
endless *va et vient.* The last was a sturdy little
boy who came and banged down a penny, and
in a wonderful bass voice for his size cried,
' Bull's-eyes.' Deborah, in imitation of his style,
banged down a ready pennyworth of bull's-eyes,
then banged the penny into an iron-basin, then
dashed back and hacked away at her steak.
' Oh dear ! ' said she, ' I wish a shilling would
come in and then a lull, instead of this continual
torrent of fiery, untamed farthing pieces.' She
hadn't half finished her steak when Mrs. Mansell and Pinder came home.

' How is he now ? ' was Sarah's first word.

'Sober as a judge, and gone out for a job; and if it is all the same to everybody, I ask just ten minutes' peace to eat my supper.' Then Deborah caught up the tray and fled into the kitchen.

She had not gone long when a detective in plain clothes looked in, and said in a low voice there was news. A female detective had been put on to Varney with rare success: she had listened in the bar of an eating-house, and had picked up the whole story—the kitchen was deserted every night; the servant was out gallivanting; Varney had come in through the kitchen and robbed the till, and to-night he was going to rob the safe or something.

'Now,' said Steele, 'get my men in without the servant knowing, and then send her out, and we shall nab the bloke to a certainty.'

Pinder acquiesced, but Sarah began to exhibit weakness. 'Oh dear!' said she, 'thieves and police, and perhaps pistols!'

Steele whispered to Pinder, 'Get her out of the way, or she'll spill the treacle.' Pinder persuaded her to go into James's room with the child until they should send for her. She consented very readily. Then Steele let in a policeman, and him behind a screen in the parlour. Two more were hidden in an empty house opposite, watching every move. Then Pinder put up the shutters and darkened the shop. Now the question was how to get Deborah out of the house. Pinder had to go and ask Sarah if she could manage that. 'In a minute,' said she. She came down, and went into the kitchen with ten shillings, and told Deborah she should have her print gown in spite of them all. Then Deborah was keen to get out before the shops closed, and in due course the confederates heard her go out and bang the kitchen door.

Now there was no saying positively whether Varney was on the watch or not; and if he was, he might make his attempt in a few minutes, or wait an hour or two. And as he was an old hand, he would probably look all round the house to see if there was danger. Every light had to be put out and the shutters drawn, and the screen carefully placed.

They closed the parlour-door, and hid in the parlour.

'But how is my man to get in?' Sarah whispered.

One of the black, undistinguishable figures replied to her, 'Easy enough, only I hope he won't come this two hours; he would spoil all.'

'Not come to his supper! Then that will be a sign he is not sober. I'm all of a tremble.'

'Hush!'

'What—thieves?'

'No; but pray don't talk. He'll come in like a cat, you may be sure. Hark!'

'What is it?'

'The kitchen-window,' whispered Steele.

Now Sarah was silent, but panted audibly in the darkness.

By-and-by a step was heard on the stairs. Then silence—another creaking step. The watchers huddled behind the screen.

What now took place they could only divine in part.

But I will describe it from the other side of the parlour-door.

A man opened the kitchen-door softly, and stepped in lightly and noiselessly as a cat.

He had a dark lantern, and flashed it one half-moment to show him the place. In that moment was revealed a face with a very small black mask. Small as it was, it effectually disguised the man, and. made his eyes look terrible with the excitement of crime. He opened the parlour-door, flashed his light in for a moment, then closed the door. That was a trying moment to the watchers. They feared he would examine the room.

Then the man stepped softly to the kitchen-door, opened it, and whispered, 'Coast clear; come on!' Another man came in on tiptoe. The first comer handed him the light.

'No,' whispered the other, 'you hold the light. Give me the key.'

Then the first comer opened the bull's-eye

direct on the safe, and gave the second man a bright new key, evidently forged for this job. The safe was opened by the second man. He looked, and uttered an ejaculation of surprise. Then he plunged his hands in, and there was a musical clatter that was heard and understood in the next room, and the watchers stole out softly.

'Here's a haul!' cried the man. 'Come and reckon 'em on the counter. Why, there's more than fifty, I know.' He put them down in a heap on the counter, and instantly the parlour-door opened, and a powerful bull's-eye shot its light upon the glittering coin. The man stood dumbfounded. The other, with a yell, dashed at the kitchen-door, tore it open, and received the fire of another bull's-eye from the foot of the stairs. He staggered back, and in a moment was at the shop-door, and opened it; the key was in it, that James might be admitted if he came. Another bull's-eye met him _there_, held by a policeman, who stepped in, and bade his mate remain outside.

The shop was now well lighted with all these vivid gleams concentrated on the stolen gold, and every now and then playing upon the masked faces and ghastly cheeks and glittering eyes of the burglars.

Steele surveyed his trapped vermin grimly for a moment or two.   He felt escape was impossible :

'Now, Dick Varney,' said he, 'you are wanted.   Handcuff him.'   The smaller figure made no resistance.   'Now who's your pal? Don't know him by his cut.   Come, my man, off with that mask, and show us your ugly mug.' He was going to help him off with it ; but the man caught up a knife that Deborah had left on the counter.'

' Touch me if you dare ! '

' Oh, that's the game, is it ? ' said Steele, sternly.   ' Draw staves, men.   Now don't you try that game with me, my bloke.   Fling down that knife, and respect the law, or you'll lie on that floor with your skull split open.'   The man flung the knife down savagely.   ' And now who are you ? '

The man tore his mask off with a snarl of rage :

'I'M THE MASTER OF THE HOUSE!'

He rang these words out like a trumpet. A faint moan was heard in the parlour.

'Gammon!' said Steele, contemptuously.

'Ask Dick Varney, ask Joe Pinder there,' said the man. 'Ask anybody.'

'Ask nobody but me,' said the miserable wife, coming suddenly forward. 'He is my husband, sir, and God help me!'

'D'ye hear?' cried the raging villain, mortified to the core, yet exultant in his revenge : 'This house is *mine*—this shop is *mine*—that woman is *mine*—and this money is *mine*.' He clutched the gold, and put it insolently into his breeches pockets. 'Take your hand off that man, Bobby.'

'Not likely,' said Steele. 'A thief caught in the act.'

'A thief! Why, he is my servant, doing my business, under my orders—*one* of my servants. My wife there—she's my servant in law—collared my money and hid it away ; I ordered another of my servants to open the safe and get me back my own. He's here by my authority.'

' Why were you in masks, my bold black-guard ? ' asked Steele.

' Oh, pray don't anger him, sir,' said poor Sarah. 'Yes, James, you are the master. It was all a mistake ; we had no idea—— Oh ! ' She tottered, and put her hand to her brow.

Steele helped her to a chair. So small an incident did not interrupt her master's elo-quence. 'Respect the law, says you? Pretty limbs of the law you are, that don't know the law of husband and wife.'

Long before this Steele had seen plainly enough that he was in the wrong box. ' We know the law well enough,' said he, de-jectedly. ' It's a little one-sided, but it's the law. Come, men, loose that vagabond.'

' He shall bring an action for false im-prisonment.'

' No, he won't.'

'Why not? He has got the law on his side.'

'And we have got his little mask, and his little antecedents, on ours.'

Varney whipped out of the place, and at the same time Deborah opened the kitchen-door and stood aghast.

'Come, men,' said Steele, 'clear out; we are only making mischief between man and wife, and she'll be the sufferer, poor thing.'

'No,' said James Mansell, authoritatively. 'I'm the master, and since you have heard one story, I'll trouble you to stay and hear the other. I'm the one that is being robbed—of my money, and my wife's affections, and my good name.'

'Oh, James!' gasped Sarah, 'pray don't say so. Don't think so for a moment.'

He ignored her entirely; never looked at her; but went on to the detective: 'My wife here hid my money away from me.'

'To pay my master's rent, and make his child a lady,' put in Sarah.

'And now she and her old sweetheart there——'

'Sweetheart! I never had but thee.'

'They have put the mark of a thief on me in this town. So be it. I leave it for ever. I'm off to America.'

He marched to the street door, then turned to shoot his last dart: '*With my money*'—and he slapped his pockets—' and *my* liberty '—and he waved his hat.

'But I'll have your life,' hissed Pinder, and strode at him, with murder in his eyes.

But Sarah Mansell, who sat there crushed, and seemed scarcely sensible, bounded to her feet in a moment, and seized Pinder with incredible vigour.

'Touch him if you dare!' cried she.

And would you believe it, mates, she had no sooner stopped him effectually than she turned weaker than ever, and sank all limp against the man she had seized with a clutch of steel? Then he had nothing to do but support her faint head against his manly breast,

II

and so, arrested by woman's vigour, which is strong for a moment, and conquered by woman's weakness, which is invincible, he half led, half lifted her tenderly back to her seat. This defence of her insulter was the last feat that day of unconquerable love.

The policemen went out softly, and cast looks of manly pity behind them.

Soon after the stunning blow came the agony of an outraged, deserted, and still loving wife. But Deborah rushed in with Lucy in her arms, and forced the mother to embrace her child, then wreathed her long arms round them both, and they, being country-bred, rocked and sobbed together. Honest Joe Pinder set his face to the wall, but there his concealment ended; he blubbered aloud with all his heart.

CHAPTER V.

THE first burst of distress was followed by the torment of suspense : for several days, at Sarah's request, the friendly police watched the steamboats, to give her an opportunity of appeasing her burglar; and all this time her eye was always on the street by day, her ear ever on the watch for the music of the blackguard's step. She kept hoping something from paternal affection : why should he abandon Lucy ? *She* had never offended him.

But in time proof was brought her that he had actually levanted in a sailing vessel bound for New York.

I do not practise vivisection, and will not detail all the sufferings of an insulted and deserted wife—sufferings all the more keen that she was a woman of great spirit and rare merit, and admired for her looks and her qualities by everybody except her husband. Public sympathy was offered her: a Liverpool journal got the incident from the police, and dealt with it in a paragraph headed

EVERY MAN HIS OWN BURGLAR.

The writer of paragraphs, after the manner of his class, seasoned the dish from his own spice box. A revolver was levelled at the auto-burglar by the wife's friend; but the wife disarmed him, a circumstance the writer deplored, and hoped that, should 'sponsa-burglary' recur, even conjugal affection would respect the interests of society, and let the bullet takes its course.

Pinder read out this paragraph, or paraphrase, and translated the last sentence into the vulgar tongue. Then Deborah revelled in it. Sarah was horrified at the exposure, and indignant at a journal presuming to meddle with conjugalia. To hear her, one would infer that if a blackguard should murder his wife, it ought to be hushed up, all matters between husband and wife, good or bad, being secret and sacred, and all indictments thereon founded obtrusive, impertinent, and indelicate.

A great sorrow has often compensations that do the heart no good at the moment; but time reveals their importance, and that they would have been comforters at the time, could the sufferers have foreseen what was coming. This observation is not necessarily connected with trust in Providence; yet the good, who suffer, should consider man's inability to foresee the events of a single day, and also that they are in the hands of One before Whom what we call the future lies flat like a map along with the past and the present.

Even my own brief experience of human life has shown me the truth and value of these lines, so comforting to just men and women :

With steady mind thy course of duty run :
God never does, nor suffers to be done,
Aught but thyself wouldst do, couldst thou foresee
The end of all events so well as He.

This story is not written to support that or any other theory ; but as all its curious incidents lie before me, I cannot help being struck with the numerous conversions of evil into unexpected good which it reveals.

The immediate examples are these. In the first place, before this great and enduring grief fell on Sarah Mansell, Mr. Joseph Pinder had a natural but narrow-minded contempt for Mrs. Deborah Smart. He saw a six months' widow husband-hunting without disguise. To put it in his own somewhat rough but racy language, she raked the town every night for No. 2. But when lasting grief fell upon Sarah, he saw this imperfect widow resign her matrimonial excursions night after night, and exhaust her ingenuity to comfort her sister. Sometimes it was rough comfort, sometimes it was the indirect comfort of kindness and attention, but sometimes it was a tender sympathy he had never expected from so rough and ready a rustic. Thereupon Pinder and Deborah became friends, and as Sarah was

, grateful, though sad, this wove a threefold cord —a very strong one.

The second good result was one that even the mourning wife appreciated, because she was a mother, and looked to the future.

Seeing her deserted and in need of help, Joseph Pinder became her servant, and yet her associate. For a fair salary he threw himself into the business, and very soon improved and enlarged it. Tinned meats, soups, and fruits were just then fighting for entrance into the stomach of the prejudiced Briton. Joseph prevailed on the sisters to taste these, and select the good ones. They very soon found that amongst the trash there were some comestible treasures, such as the Boston baked beans, Australian beef briskets, and an American ox-tail soup ; also, the pears of one firm in Delaware, and the peaches of another.

Pinder, who, like many workmen, was an ingenious fellow, had invested his savings in a type-writer, and he printed short notices, and inundated inns and private kitchens with the

praises of the above articles, and personally invited many cooks and small housekeepers to the
use of his cheap American soup for gravies.
' Where,' said he, ' is the sense of your boiling
down leg of beef for gravies and stews and
things? Here are six rich stews, or hashes, for
10*d.*, and no trouble but to take it out of a can.'

One day Sarah showed him, with sorrowful
pride, James Mansell's 'panels,' as he called
them. That personage, before he took to drink,
was an enthusiast in his art, and he had produced
about fifteen specimens on thin panels two feet
square. They were really magnificent. Joseph
cleaned and varnished them; then caught a
moderate grainer, and made him study them;
then put one or two of them in a window,
with a notice: 'Graining done in first-rate
style by a pupil of Joseph Mansell.' The trade
soon heard, and gave the young man a trial.
He was not up to the mark of his predecessor,
but, thanks to the models, and Pinder over-
looking his work, he was accepted by degrees,
and so Mrs. Mansell drove her husband's trade

and her own enlarged. Money flowed in by two channels, and did not flow out for ' drink.' Pinder's salary was not one-tenth part of the increase his zeal and management brought into the safe, and now there was no drunkard and auto-burglar to drain the wife's purse and tap the till.

In the three years whose incidents I have decided not to particularise, and so be tri-voluminous, not luminous, the deserted wife had purchased the little shop and premises in Green Street, and had 400*l.* in the bank, Pinder having declared the London and County Bank to be safer than a safe.

Lucy Mansell was now over seven, and a precocious girl, partly by nature (for she came of a clever father and a thoughtful mother), but partly by living not with children, but with grown-up people. As she inherited her mother's attention, and was a born mimic, she seemed to strangers cleverer than she was. The sprightliness of Aunt Deborah naturally attracted this young person, and of course she admired what

at any young ladies' school she would have
been expressly invited to avoid—the by-words
and blunt idioms that garnished Mrs. Smart's
discourse.

Now, having faithfully, though briefly,
chronicled the small beer, I come to the events
of an exciting day.

Sarah sat at the counter, sewing, and ready
to serve customers.   Lucy sat at her knee,
sewing, and ready to run for whatever might
be wanted.   Deborah came up from the kitchen
with a rump-steak and some kidneys in her
market basket, and thrust them under her
sister's nose.   Deborah was a *connoisseur* of
raw meat, luckily for the establishment, and
admired it when good.   Sarah did not admire
it at the best of times, so she said, ' I'll take
your word.'

' Do but feel it,' persisted Deborah.   Thereupon Sarah averted her head.

Deborah warmed.   ' Wait till you see it at
table.   I am going to make you a steak-and-
kidney pudding.'

'Oh, be joyful!' cried Lucy, and clapped her hands.

'Come, there's sense in the family,' remarked Deborah; 'and if your mother doesn't enjoy it, I give warning at the table—that's all.'

'I'll try, sister,' said Sarah, sweetly. 'But you know an empty chair at the head of the table is a poor invitation to eat, and the stomach is soon satisfied when the heart is sad.'

'That is true, my poor Sal; but, dear heart, is there never to be an end of fretting for a man that left you like that, and has never sent you a line?'

'That is my grief. I am afraid he is dead.'

'Not he. He has got plenty more mischief to do first. Now I'm afraid you'll hate me, but I can't help it. "The truth may be blamed, but it can't be shamed." 'Twas the luckiest thing ever happened to any good woman when he left you, and you got a good servant instead of a bad master.'

'If I only knew that he was alive!' persisted Sarah, absorbed in her one idea.

Deborah's patience went, and she let out her real mind. She had kept it to herself about eighteen months, so now it came out with a rush. She set her arms akimbo—an attitude she very seldom adopted in reasoning with Sarah. 'If so be as you are tired of peace and comfort, and money in both pockets, you put it in the newspapers as you have bought these premises, and got 400*l.* in the bank, and you mark my words, Jemmy Mansell will turn up in a month; but 'tis for your money he will come, not for you nor your child.'

This home-thrust produced a greater effect on Sarah than Deborah expected; for as a rule Sarah merely defended her husband through thick and thin; but now she was greatly agitated, and when Deborah came to that galling conclusion, she drew herself up to her full height, and said sternly, 'If I thought that, I'd tear him from my heart, though I tore the heart out of my body. Perhaps you think because I'm single-hearted and loving, that I

am all weakness. You don't know me, then.
When I do turn, I turn to stone.'

As she said this, her features became
singularly rigid, and almost cruel, and as a
great pallor overspread them at the same time,
she really seemed to turn to marble, and the
gentle Sarah was scarcely recognisable. Even
Deborah, who had known her all her life, stared
at her, and suspected she had not yet got to the
bottom of her character. Lucy gave the conversation a lighter turn—she thought all this
was much ado about nothing. 'Don't you fret
any more, mamma,' said she. 'If papa won't
come home, you marry Uncle Joe.'

Mrs. Mansell remonstrated : 'Lucy dear, for
shame.'

> 'No shame, no sin ;
> No copper, no tin,'

said Lucy. 'Marry him bang! Here he is.'

'Hush!' and Sarah reddened like fire.

Pinder opened the shop door, and came
briskly in for business. 'Good-morning, Sarah ;
morning, Deborah ; morning, little Beauty.

Made a good collection this time. Please open your ledger and begin alphabetical. B— Bennett, the new hotel, 3*l.* 13*s.* 6*d.* There's the money.' Sarah wrote the payment off Bennett in the ledger. Pinder went on putting each payment on the counter in a separate paper. 'Church, 1*l.* 5*s.* ; Mr. Drake, 7*l.* 9*s.*'

'That's a he-duck,' suggested Lucy.

'You're another, allowing for sex,' retorted Pinder. 'And now we jump to M—Mr. Mayor.'

'That is a she-horse,' remarked Lucy, always willing to impart information. Pinder denied that, and said it was the great civic authority of the town, and in proof produced his Worship's cheque for 17*l.* 4*s.* And now what's the news here?' he enquired.

'I'll tell you,' said miss, with an obliging air. 'Mamma and Aunt Deb have just had a shindy.'

'Oh, fie!' cried Deborah. 'It's you for picking up expressions.'

'Then why do you let them fall?' said the

mother. ' It's you she copies. We only
differed in opinion.'

' And bawled at one another,' suggested
Lucy.

Deborah exclaimed, ' Oh, for shame, to say
that ! '

Says this terrible child : ' " The truth may
be blamed, but it can't be shamed." You know
you did.'

' It sounds awful,' said Pinder, drily. ' Let
us make 'em friends again. What is the row?'
and Mr. Pinder grinned incredulous.

' Well,' explained Lucy, in spite of a furtive
signal from her mother, ' mamma fretted because papa does not write ; then *she* '—(point-
ing at Deborah, *malgré* the rules of good
breeding)—'quarrelled her for fretting, and she
said, " You put it in the papers how rich you
are, and he'll turn up directly." Then mamma
bounced up and gave it her hot '—(Sarah
scandalised, Deborah amused)—' and then it
ended with mamma crying. Everything ends
with poor mamma crying.' Then Lucy flung

her arms round her mother's neck, and Pinder
suggested, 'Little angel.'

Sarah kissed her child tenderly, and said,
'No—no quarrel. And do but give me proof
that he is alive, and I'll never shed another tear.'

'Is that a bargain?' asked Pinder, quietly.

'That it is.'

'Just give me your hand upon it then.'
She gave him her hand and looked eagerly in
his face.

He walked out of the shop directly, as-
sailed by a fire of questions, to none of which
he replied. The truth is he could not at
present promise anything. But he knew this
much; that Dick Varney had gone out to New
York three months ago, and had been seen at
a public-house in the neighbourhood of Green
Street that very day. Pinder got it into his
head that Varney would most likely know
whether Mansell was alive or dead. With
some difficulty he found Varney. That worthy
was dilapidated, so he was induced by the
promise of a sovereign to come and tell Mrs.

Mansell all he knew about her husband. The sly Varney objected to tell Pinder until he had fingered the money, and asked for an advance. This the wary Pinder declined peremptorily, but showed him the coin.

Thus distrusting each other, they settled to go to Green Street. But when he got to the door, Varney remembered the scene of the burglary, and the woman's distress; he took fright and wanted to go back.

'No, no,' said Pinder; 'I'll bear the blame of this visit,' and almost forced him in.

The family was still all in a flutter, and Deborah bearing her sister company in the shop. Though Sarah had only seen Varney once, his face and figure were indelible in her memory, and at the sight of him she gave a faint scream, put both her hands before her face, and turned her head away into the bargain. 'Oh, that man!' she cried.

'There!' said Varney, 'she can't bear the sight of me, and no wonder.' With this remark—the most creditable he had made for

I

years—he tried to bolt. But Pinder collared him, and held him tight, and for the first time this three years scolded Sarah. 'Why, where's the sense of flying at the man, and frightening what little courage he has out of him, and shutting his mouth?'

'No, no,' said Deborah, hastily, 'if you can tell her anything about her man, don't you doubt your welcome. Let bygones be bygones.'

'I am bound to answer whatever *she* asks me.'

'And I'm bound to give you this, if you do,' said Pinder. 'Deborah shall hold it meantime.' He handed over the sovereign to Deborah. Her fingers closed on it, and did not seem likely to open without the equivalent.

During all this Sarah's eyes had been gradually turning round toward the man, and by a feminine change they now dwelt on him as if they would pierce him.

'You have been to New York?'

'Yes.'

CHAPTER VI.

'DID you look for my husband?'

'You may be sure of that, and it took me all my time to find him.'

'Find him! He is alive?'

'Alive! Of course he is.'

'Thank God! thank God!'

She was so overcome that Pinder and Deborah came to her assistance, but she waved them off. 'No,' said she, 'joy won't hurt me. Alive and well?'

'Never better.'

'And happy?'

'Jolly as a sand-boy.'

'A sand-boy?' murmured Lucy, enquiringly.

Sarah's next question was uttered timidly and piteously—'Did he ask after us?'

Deborah cast an uneasy glance at Pinder. She was sorry her sister had asked that, and feared a freezing reply.

'Rather,' said Varney.   'First word he said was, "How is Sarah and the kid?"'

'Bless him!' cried Sarah.   'Bless him!'

Lucy informed the company that a kid was a little goat.

But her innocence did not provoke a smile. They were all hanging on Dick Varney's words.

'And what did *you* say about us?'

'Oh, well, I could only tell him what I hear of all sides, that you are doing his trade as well as your own.   That Joe Pinder is your factotum.   That you are as rich as a Jew, and respected accordingly.'

'You told him that?' said Deborah, keenly.

'Those were my very words.'

'And he didn't come back with you?' she asked.

'No.'

'Then he must be doing well out there?'

'I shouldn't wonder; he was dressed like a gentleman.'

'And he looked like one, I'll be bound,' said his devoted wife.

'He didn't behave like one, then, for he gave an old friend the cold shoulder.'

'What a pity!' suggested Deborah—'you that used to set him such a good example.'

Pinder said that was not fair, and the man telling them all he could. Deborah said no more it wasn't, and if Mr. Varney would come with her, she would cook him a bit of this nice steak.

He said he should be very glad of it.

'But mind, there's no brandy allowed in this house. Can you drink home-brewed ale?'

'I can drink anything,' said he, eagerly.

She showed him into the kitchen, but whipped back again for a moment. 'There's more behind than he has told *you*,' said she. 'I'm a-going to pump him.' She ran off again directly ·to carry out this design, and very capable of it she was: just the sort of woman

to wait for him like a cat, and go about the
bush, and put no question of any importance
till he had eaten his fill, and drunk the home-
brewed ale, which tasted innocent, but was
very heady. This manœuvre of hers raised
some vague expectations in the grown-up
people, but Lucy's mind, as usual, fixed itself
on a word.

'Pump him?' said she to Pinder. 'How
will she do that, Factotum?'

'Not knowing, can't say,' was Factotum's
reply.

'Like this, Factotum?' said she, and took
his arm and pumped with it. 'Good-bye,
Factotum,' said she, for a new word was like a
new toy to her; 'I'm off to see the pumping.'

Pinder laughed and looked at Sarah; but
not a smile. 'Why, you are not going to fret
again?' said he. 'You gave me your word to
be happy if he was alive.'

'And I thought I should at the time. But
now I know he is alive, I know too that he is
dead to me. Alive all this time, and not write

me a line! I insulted him, and he hates me. I'm a deserted wife.'

'And I am a useless friend. Nothing I do is any use.' He lost heart for a time, and went and took a turn in the street, despondent, and for the moment a little out of temper.

She watched his retiring figure, and thought he had gone for good, and felt that she must appear ungrateful, and should wear out this true friend's patience before long. 'I can't help it,' said she to herself. 'I can love but one, and him I shall never see again.'

Never was her sense of desolation so strong as at that moment. She laid her brow on the counter, and her tears ran slowly but steadily.

She had been so some time when a voice somewhere near her said, rather timidly, 'Sally.'

She lifted her head a little way from the counter, but did not look toward where the voice came from; it seemed liked a sound in a dream to her.

'It is,' said the man, and came quickly to her. Then she looked and uttered a scream of rapture, and in a moment husband and wife were locked in each other's arms.

At this moment Pinder, whose momentary impatience had very soon given way to compassion and pity, came back to make the *amende* by increased kindness; and Deborah, who knew every tone of her sister's voice, flew up from the kitchen at her cry of joy.   But in the first rapture of meeting and reconciliation neither spouse took any notice of these astounded witnesses.

'My Jemmy! my own! my own!'

'My sweet, forgiving wife!'

'It is me should ask forgiveness.'

'No, no!   'Twas the police drove me mad.'

'To leave me for three years!'

'Do you think I'd have stayed away three weeks if I had thought I should be so welcome?'

'What! you did not know how I love you?'

Then came another embrace, and at last Sarah realised that there were two spectators, one on each side of her, and those spectators

not so much in love with the recovered treasure
as she was. She said, 'Come, dearest, joy is
sacred,' and drew him by both hands, with
a deal of grace and tenderness, into the little
parlour, and closed the door.

Pinder and Deborah looked at each other
long and expressively, and by an instinct of
sympathy met at the counter as soon as the
parlour door closed, Deborah very red, and her
eyes glittering, Pinder ghastly pale.

'Well, Mr. Pinder,' said she, with affected
calm, but ill-concealed bitterness, 'you and
I—we are two nobodies now. Three years'
kindness of our side goes for nothing, and three
years' desertion don't count against him. I've
heard that absence makes the heart grow
fonder,' and now 'tis to be seen.'

Pinder apologised for his idol. 'She can't
help it,' said he. 'But I can help looking on.
I've seen them meet, after him abandoning her
this three years, and what I feel this moment
will last me all my time. I won't stay to watch
them together, like the devil grinning at Adam

and Eve ; and I won't wait to hear him say that this business I have enlarged is *his*, the trade that he killed and I have revived is *his*, that the woman is *his*, and the child is *his*, and the money we have saved is *his*. No, Deborah, I'll give her my blessing and go, soon as ever I have put up those shutters for her, and it is about time. You will see Joseph Pinder in this place no more.'

'What, you will desert her and all?'

'Desert her? That is not the word. I leave her when she is happy. I am only her friend in trouble.'

'And not her friend in danger, then?'

'I see no danger just at present.'

'Think a bit, my man. What has brought him home? Answer me that.'

'Well, I can,' said he. 'There is plenty of attraction to bring any man home that is not blind, and mad, and an idiot.'

'Ay,' said she, 'that is how you look at her ; but it's him I want you to read. Why, it was three years since he left, but it's not a

month since that Varney told him she was a
rich woman, and here he is directly.'

' Oh ! ' said honest Joe Pinder. ' I see what
you are driving at ; but that may be accidental.
Things fall together like that. We mustn't be
bad-hearted neither. Why, surely he can't be
so base ! '

' He is no worse than he was, and no better,
you may be sure. Crossing the water can't
change a man's skin, nor his heart neither, and
I tell you he has come here disguised as a
gentleman for the thing he came for disguised
as a burglar.'

Here she tapped the safe with the key of
the kitchen-door, which she had in her hand,
and that action and the ring of the metal made
her reasoning tell wonderfully. She followed
up her advantage, and assured Pinder that if
he did not stay and lend her his support, Sarah
would soon be stripped bare, and then abandoned again.

' If he does,' said Pinder, ' I'll kill him,
that is all.'

'With all my heart,' was Deborah's reply.
'But you mustn't leave *her*. And then,' said
she, 'there's *me*. You that is so good-natured,
would you leave me to fight against the pair?
To be sure, I am cook, and my kitchen is over-
run with rats; and one penn'orth of white
arsenic would rid the place of them and the
two-legged vermin and all.'

Pinder was shocked, and begged her
solemnly never to harbour such thoughts for
a moment.

'Then don't you leave me alone with my
thoughts,' said she, 'for I hate him with all my
heart and soul.'

The discussion did not end there; and, to
be brief, Deborah had the best of it to the end.
Pinder, however, was for once doggedly resolved to consider his own feelings as well as
Sarah's interests. He would go; but consented
not to leave the town, and to look in occasion-
ally just to see whether Sarah was being pillaged.

'But,' said he, 'if 'tis all one to you, I will
come to the kitchen, not the shop.'

The ready-witted Deborah literally and without a metaphor licked her lips at him when he proposed this, so hearty was her appetite for a *tête-à-tête* or two in her own kitchen with this Joseph Pinder; he had pleased her eye from the first moment she saw him.

She said: 'Well, so do. "What the eye don't see the heart don't grieve." Leave him the shop, and you come in the kitchen.'

With this understanding Pinder put up the shutters and went away, sick at heart. Deborah had half a mind to stay in her kitchen, so odious to her was the sight of her brother-in-law; and, besides, she was jealous; however, her courage was a quality that came and went. She was afraid to declare war on the pair, with nobody on the spot to back her. So she temporised; she took Lucy into the parlour to welcome her father. The child said, 'How d'ye do, papa?' in rather an off-hand way, and was kissed overflowingly. She did not respond one bit, and began immediately to fire questions : ' Why did you go away so long, and make mamma fret ? Why didn't you write to her, if you couldn't come ? '

Sarah stopped the rest of the cross-examination with her hand, and told Lucy it was not for her to question her father. Deborah never moved a muscle, but chuckled inwardly.

' What will you have for supper, now that you are come ? ' inquired she, with affected graciousness.

' Anything you like,' said James, politely. ' Don't make a stranger of me.'

That evening the reunited couple spent in sweet reminiscences and the renewal of conjugal ardour.

Before morning, however, they had talked of everything—at all events, Sarah had, and being grateful to Pinder, and anxious to make her benefactor and her husband friends, had revealed the results of Joseph's faithful service and intelligence—the shop purchased, and 440*l.* in the bank.

' At what interest ? ' inquired James.

'Oh, no interest. I am waiting to buy land or a good house with it.'

James laughed, and said that was England all over—to let money lie dead for which ten per cent. could be had in the United States on undeniable security.

When once he got upon this subject he was eloquent; descanted on the vast opportunities offered both to industry and capital in the United States; bade her observe how he had improved his condition by industry alone.

'But with capital,' said he, 'I could soon make you a lady.'

'Lucy you might,' said she, 'but I shall live and die a simple woman.'

Finding she listened to him, he returned to the subject again and again; but I do not think it necessary to give the dialogue *in extenso*. There is a certain monotony in the eloquence of speculation, and the sensible objections of humdrum prudence. I spare the reader these, having sworn not to be tri-voluminous.

It was about twelve o'clock next day when Pinder, whose occupation was gone, and *ennui* and deadness of heart substituted, found the time so heavy on his hands that he must come and chat with Deborah in her kitchen. He looked in; she was not there. So then he peeped in timidly at the shop window, and there she was in sole possession of the counter. Her qualifications for that post were as well known to him as to the readers of this tale, so he looked surprised.

'Why, where are they all?'

'In Cupid's Bower,' said Deborah, repeating a phrase out of a daily paper. 'Billing and cooing are sweeter than business.'

'Where's Lucy?'

'You are the first that has asked. Well, she is asleep upstairs. My lady found herself neglected first time this three years, so she came and cried to me, and I took her in my arms and laid her on the bed. She's all right. Pity grown-up people can't go to sleep when they like and forget.'

At this moment the parlour-door opened, and Sarah Mansell, who had worn nothing but black these three years, emerged beaming in a blue dress with white spots, and a lovely bonnet, all gay and charming. This bright vision banished Deborah's discontent in a moment. 'Well,' said she, 'you *are* a picture.' Sarah stopped to be looked at, and smiled.

'Well,' said Deborah, 'he has found a way to make us all glad he is come home.'

Sarah smiled affectionately on her, and said she only wished she could make everybody as happy as she was.

'Why not?' said Deborah, playing the courtier to please her. 'And where are you going so pert, I wonder?'

'To the bank to draw my money,' replied Sarah, gaily.

Pinder and Deborah looked at one another.

'How much of it?' asked Deborah.

'Four hundred pounds,' said the wife, brightly.

K

Pinder groaned, but was silent. Deborah threw up her hands.

'Oh, Sarah,' said she piteously, ' do but think how long it has taken you to make that, and don't throw it into a well all at one time.'

Sarah smiled superior. 'I affronted him about money three years ago, and you see what came of it.'

She was going out jauntily, neither angry nor in any way affected by her friends' opposition, when Pinder put in a serious word.

'Well,' said he, ' give him a good slice. But do pray leave a little for Lucy. You are a mother as well as a wife.'

She turned on him at the door with sudden wrath to crush him with a word for daring to teach her her duty as a mother; then she remembered all she owed him, and restrained herself. But what a look flashed from her eyes! And the hot blood mounted to her temples.

Pinder was quite staggered at such a look from her, and Deborah shook her head. They both felt they were nullities, and James Mansell the master again. He let them know it, too. He had been quietly listening on the stairs to every word they had said to his wife, and he now stepped into the shop and took up a commanding position on the public side of the counter, opposite Pinder and Deborah. They were standing behind the counter at some distance from each other.

It was Pinder he attacked: said he, quietly, 'Are you going to meddle again between man and wife? It didn't answer last time, did it?'

Pinder did not think it advisable to quarrel if it could be helped, so he said not a word.

But Deborah was not so discreet. 'Why, you have allowed him to meddle this three years. *You* pillaged and deserted her; *he* interfered, and made her fortune. He doesn't meddle to mar.'

Then Pinder spoke, but in a more pacific tone. 'I don't want to meddle at all,' said he. 'But Deborah and I have done our best for you both, and I do think your wife's friends might be allowed to ask what is to be done in one day with the savings of three years.' Before these words were out of his mouth Mansell registered a secret vow to get rid of him and Deborah both.

He replied, with the intention of galling them to the quick, 'Well, I don't know that the master is bound to tell the servants what he does with his money.'

' *Your* money?' snorted Deborah.

' Ay,' said this imperturbable person. 'My wife's money is mine. I thought I had made you understand that last time. Well, what I am going to do with my money is to invest it in American securities at ten per cent., instead of letting it lie idle in an English bank.'

'Oh!' said Deborah. 'That is the tale you have been telling her, eh? Well, I mean to tell her the truth. You are going to collar her money and off to America directly. Varney has been here, and split on you. You came for the money, not the woman.'

She flung these words in his face so violently
that even his brazen cheek flushed as if she
had struck him; but ere he could reply, Sarah
stood aghast in the doorway. ' Oh dear! high
words already.'

Then James Mansell, who, in his way, was
cleverer than any of them, recovered his composure in a moment, and said, quietly: ' Not
on my side, I assure you. But this young
woman says I have come for your money, not
for you. That's a pretty thing to bawl at a
man for all the street to hear. Well, Sarah, I
don't bawl at *her*, but I put it to *you* quietly—
how can I live in the same house with people
that hate me, and are on the watch to poison
my wife's mind against me?'

CHAPTER VII.

PINDER and Deborah both felt they had met their match. Pinder held his peace ; but Deborah couldn't. Her lips trembled, but she fought him to the last. 'I shall leave this house at one word from my sister ; but not at the bidding of a stranger that's here to-day and gone to-morrow, as soon as he has milked the cow and bled the calf.' With a grand sweeping gesture of the left arm she indicated Sarah as the cow, and with her right, Lucy as the calf.

The tremendous words, and the vulgar yet free and large gestures with which she drove them home, made even Pinder say, 'Oh !' and so upset Mansell's cunning self-command that he came at her furiously. But Sarah stopped him. ' No, you shall not answer her, James.

You go and take your daughter on your knee, and I'll tell these two my mind.' She was so grave and dignified there was no resistance.

Mansell retired with Lucy, and went up the stairs.

When he was quite gone, Sarah put out her two hands and said, sweetly, ' Come here, you two.' Then they each took a hand, and their eyes glistened.

She took them gently to task in silvery accents, that calmed and soothed them as they fell. ' You have a true affection for me, both of you. Then pity me, too, and don't drive me into a corner. Do not make me choose between my husband and you; you know which I *must* choose. Why, dear heart, if I spent my money on my back, you would not grudge it me. Then why not let me please my heart, and give my money where I give my love, that is worth more than 400*l.* if you could but see it.'

They were both subdued by her words.

Deborah said, in a sort of broken, helpless way to Pinder, 'She doesn't understand.'

'What we mean is that if you part with your money, you will lose your man; but so long as you stick to your money, he will stay with you; and we have both seen how you can fret for him when he does desert you as well as bleed you.'

'Ay,' said Sarah, nobly, and without anger. 'You mean me well; but you doubt, and mistrust, and suspect. No offence to either of you, but your nature is not mine. I am single-hearted. I cannot love and mistrust. Nor I could not mistrust and love.'

The beauty of her mind and the sweetness of her strong but sober words overpowered her old lover and tender friend. 'Don't harass her any more,' said he. 'She is too good for this world. She is an angel.'

Deborah smiled, and after taking a good look at her sister, said, coolly, 'She is a wonderful good woman; her face would tell one that; but she *is* a woman, you may be sure,

like her mother before her. Sarah, 'tis no use
beating about the bush any longer. Would
you like that 400*l.* to go to another woman ? '

'Another woman ? ' cried the supposed
angel, firing up directly. 'What do you mean ?
What other woman ? '

'Dick Varney saw him with a woman, and
a handsome one.'

'Well, what does that prove ? '

'Not much by itself; but a man that leaves
one woman for three years, at his time of life, is
safe to take on with another.'

'Oh ! ' cried Sarah, 'don't tell me so.'

But Deborah was launched. She said : ' It's
all a mystery, and against nature, if there's no
other woman ; but, if there's another, it's all as
plain as a pikestaff. Three years' dead silence
and neglect—another woman—you fretting in
England—no other man—(Mr. Pinder is only a
friend)—he jolly as a sand-boy in New York—
another woman—*she* wants money (t'other
woman always does)—Dick Varney tells *him*
you've got it—he's here in one month after

that, and the first day he is here he drains
the cow.   American insecurities ?—A Yankee
gal !'

This time her rude eloquence and homely
sense carried all before them.   Sarah, whose
face had changed with the poison of jealousy,
lost all her Madonna-like calmness.   She was
almost convulsed ; she moaned aloud : 'If it
is so, Heaven help me !'   She put her hand to
her bosom, and her beautiful brown eyes half
disappeared upward and showed an excess of
white.   ' Oh, sister, you have put a viper in my
bosom—doubt.   It will gnaw away my heart.'

' Heaven forbid !' cried Deborah, terrified at
her sister's words, and still more at her strange
looks.   Then she began to blame her woman's
tongue, and beg Sarah to dismiss her suspicions
with contempt.   But this was met by another
change, almost as remarkable in its way. 'No,'
said Sarah, with iron firmness, 'I could not
love, and doubt, and live.   I'll put it to the
test.'   Deborah looked amazed and puzzled.
Sarah walked to the parlour-door and called

up the stairs, 'James, dear, please come here.'
'Whatever will she do or say?' groaned
Deborah, and began to shiver. Sarah came
back to her, and said, in a sort of hissing
whisper, 'Now, since you have taught me to
suspect, and distrust, and doubt, you must go a
little farther. I bid you watch my husband's
face, and his very body, whilst I, that am his
wife, play upon him.' She hung her head,
ashamed of what she was going to do. But
Deborah said, roughly, 'Won't I—that's all.'

James Mansell came in, and cast a shrewd
glance all round. Deborah's face told him
nothing. She wore an expression of utter
indifference. Pinder hung his head.

Mansell was now between two masked
batteries; his wife's eyes scanned him point-
blank, and Deborah watched him—like a cat—
out of the tail of her eye, as Sarah tested her
husband.

'James, dear, I have a great affection for
my sister, and a true respect for Joseph Pinder, and I owe them both a debt of gratitude.'

James looked rather gloomy at that. ' But I love you better than all the world. I can't bear to turn these faithful friends out of the house ; they comforted me when I was desolate.' Mansell looked dark again. ' And yet I can't have you made uncomfortable for anybody. So, if my company is as welcome to you as my money, we will go to America together.'

Pinder and Deborah both uttered exclamations of surprise and dismay, but Deborah's eye never left James. He was startled, but showed no reluctance. He merely said, ' You don't mean that ? '

' Indeed I do ; but perhaps you don't want me. You would rather go back alone.'

The four eyes watched.

' No,' said James ; ' we have been parted long enough. But would you really cross the water with me ? '

' As I would cross this room, if you really wanted me.'

' Of course I want you, if we are not to

live together here, where your friends hate me.
But, Sally, if you are game to emigrate with
me, why make two bites of a cherry? We
must sell the shop and realise, and settle in
the States for life. I've no friends here, and
you'll never want to come to England again,
when once you have spent a summer in New
York.'

Here was a poisoned arrow. Deborah
clasped her hands piteously, and cried, ' Oh,
Sarah.'

Sarah put up one hand to her to be quiet.

'No,' said she, as shortly and drily as if
she was chopping fire-wood, ' I'll not fling my
sister on the world, nor put all my Lucy's eggs
in one basket. I will risk 400*l*. and no more.
I don't look to find the streets of New York
city paved with gold. Money must be lost by
one for another to make it, and the folk out
there are as sharp as we are—sharper by all
accounts. Many go there for wool, and come
back shorn. This shop is a little haven for
us, if things go wrong out there. These good

friends will keep it warm for us.   Now I think
of it, doesn't a boat start for New York this
evening?'

'This evening!' cried Pinder and Deborah
in one breath.

'Ay, this very night—before affection is
soured by disputes, and love is poisoned by
jealousies.'   Then she told James to put on his
hat, and bring her word when the boat started.
Lucy and she would be ready; she could pack
all her clothes in half-an-hour, with Deborah to
help.   Thus the greater character asserted itself
at last.   She had seen with a woman's readiness
that the present position was untenable for a
day, and she had cut the knot with all a man's
promptitude.   From that hour she took the lead.

Deborah was wringing her hands and crying: 'Oh, what have I said?   What have I
done?'

Sarah said, quietly, 'Time will show.   Please
come and help me pack; and, Joseph, put up
the shutters; I trade no more this day.   Ah,
well, I never thought to leave home; but no

matter. A wife's home is by her husband's side.'

Whilst they were packing, and Deborah's tears bursting out every now and then, Sarah said to her, a little haughtily, 'Well, did he stand the test?'

'Yes,' said Deborah, humbly.

'Do you think he would take me to New York if there was another woman?'

'No' (very humbly).

'But see,' said she, sorrowfully, 'what it is to rouse mistrust. I shall sew the notes into his Sunday waistcoat, but I shall not give them to him until we are on the sea.'

Deborah began to say, 'And why—' but she got no further. She ended with 'I'm afraid to speak.'

They got the man's Sunday waistcoat out of the drawer, and their quick fingers soon cut a deep inside pocket. Sarah took the numbers of the notes, and sewed in the notes themselves. They packed the waistcoat for the time being at the bottom of Sarah's box.

The packing was done two hours before the vessel sailed.

The whole party met again in the parlour —Pinder to bid good-bye; but Mansell, to please his wife, I suppose, said, civilly: ' No, no; come and see us on board. There let us part friends; the chances are you will never see us again.'

These words fell like a knell on the true hearts Sarah Mansell left behind her.

Pinder and Deborah saw the Mansells go down the Mersey, and returned sadly to the house that had lost its sunshine.

That night Deborah, all in tears, begged Pinder not to leave her alone in the house. She said she could not bear to talk of anybody but Sarah; if she went out her friends would chatter about this, that, and t'other.

Pinder was of the same mind, and gladly embraced the proposal. She gave him his choice of Lucy's room or the connubial chamber. He gave a little shudder, and chose Lucy's. He now became the master of the house and the

shop, and had plenty on his hands. He taught
Deborah the prices of things, and how to weigh
and put up goods in paper, and that is an art;
and at night he read her a journal or a book,
and they talked of Sarah, and wondered and
wondered what would be her fate. Deborah
thought she would come back in about a year.
The 400*l.* would not last longer than that in
Mansell's hands, and he would be sure to get
hold of it. But Pinder thought she would not
return at all. James Mansell was evidently
jealous of her friends, and determined to have
her all to himself.

There was a very good photograph of her
—cabinet size; he took this to Ferranti, and
had it enlarged, retouched, and tinted by that
artist. Ferranti, who employed a superior
hand to retouch these enlargements under his
own eye, produced a marvel. It had the
solidity and clean outline of a statue.

They had it lightly tinted, especially the eyes
and hair, so as not to injure the transparency

L

of the photograph; and there was Sarah Mansell, full size, and all but alive.

It arrived, quite finished, rather late at night, and Pinder was out; but he opened the case and took it out, and neither he nor Deborah could go to bed for gazing at it. 'I never knew how beautiful she was,' said Deborah. They actually sat up till two o'clock looking at this reproduction of a good and beautiful face, and they descanted on her virtues, and Deborah told incidents of her childhood, and Pinder repeated wise and sober answers from her sweet lips.

Pinder now found himself gliding from bachelor life into half-matrimonial. His dinner was always ready on a clean cloth; and a comely woman, a year younger than himself, cooked it, and put on a clean apron and cap to eat with him. They supped together, too. She gave up her nightly excursions after a husband, and was always at his service, and ready to talk to him or listen to him, or both;

for if he read aloud police cases, or other things in which men and women revealed their characters and the broad features of human nature, her comments were as sagacious—especially in relation to her own sex—as if she had devoted her life to the study of philosophy.

Sometimes, too, she had a look of her sister. He never expected to see Sarah any more, and, take it altogether, he was on the road which, by a gentle incline, has often led the victim of a romantic attachment to a quiet union of affection.

When they were fairly out at sea, Sarah brought James his waistcoat, and showed him how the notes were secured. 'You keep them,' said she, ' and I keep the numbers.'

Mansell's greedy eyes flashed. ' Well, you are a business woman ; we shall never go wrong together.'

The water was like glass for eight days, but then they had a gale, and Mansell was very ill. It was calm again as they drew near the end

of their voyage; but Mansell did not regain
his looks. When they reached the port he
looked ill, pale, depressed, and worried.

They landed, and left their boxes in the
Custom-house, and James Mansell told Sarah
and Lucy to stay there, whilst he ran into a
neighbouring street to see whether his old
lodgings—very comfortable ones—were vacant.

She called after him not to be long:
' Mind, I am strange here,' said she.

' He won't be long, I guess,' said a civil
officer standing by; then he brought two
chairs.

' Thank you kindly, sir,' said she. ' Lucy,
my dear, thank the gentleman.' Lucy took
the two steps her dancing-master prescribed as
essential preliminaries of a curtsey, and then
effected a prim reverence—' Thank you, sir.'

The gentleman, a tall, gaunt citizen from
Illinois, grinned, and struck a bow, with his
hat in his hand, at right angles.

Sarah watched her husband take the second
street to the right and disappear. Then she

took out some work, not to be idle, and Lucy prattled away, all admiration. Never had this brilliant city a more appreciative critic. To be sure, she had not learned the suicidal habit of detraction, thanks to which nothing pleases us, and so we pick up nothing.

An hour passed—two hours—James did not come back. Sarah was mortified—then she was perplexed—then she was alarmed. What if he had gone drinking! He seemed exhausted by the voyage. Once this fear took possession of her, waiting there idle became intolerable to her. She begged that civil officer to put their boxes aside for a time, and she took Lucy by the hand and followed in the direction her husband had taken. But as she walked for hours before she found her treasure, I ask leave to go before her to a certain street.

CHAPTER VIII.

SOLOMON B. GRACE, the man who was so civil
to Sarah Mansell at the Custom-house, was, in
nis way, a rough and sturdy example of the
species Pinder ; and on his way to and from
the Custom-house he used always to stand
stock-still for two minutes and gaze at the windows of a house in One-hundred-and-fourth
Street, that belonged to one Elizabeth Haynes.
Two minutes is not long for a busy man to
spare to the past, and Solomon had never been
detected at the weakness. But to-day Elizabeth Haynes caught sight of him as she put
on her bonnet at a glass to go out, and when
she did come out at the door there he was
gazing at the windows.

Mrs. Haynes was a handsome, gay young
woman, of a genial disposition. She knew very

well what Solomon was up to, but useless sentiment was not her line.

'Well,' said she, feigning astonishment, ' is
that you, Mr. Grace, standing there like a
petrified policeman?' Solomon was too con-
founded to answer. 'Perhaps you want apart-
ments;' and she pointed to the card in the
window.

'Perhaps I wanted a sight of the lady that
lets 'em.'

'Then why not knock at the door and ask
for the lady?'

'Wa'al, I guess rejected suitors ain't always
the most welcome callers.'

'Why not? If they behave themselves, do
you really think any woman hates a man for
having been a little sweet on her? Next time
don't watch the premises, but walk right in and
tell me the news from out West.'

'Wa'al,' said he, hesitating, 'ye see, I don't
want no fuss. Now there's somebody in that
house that riles me. He has got a good thing,
and doesn't vally it. He gambles away all your

money, and he is never at home. You were married to one Illinois man, and he respected you and loved you ; and what mad dog bit you that you must go and marry a stranger? You had the whole State to pick from.'

'And Mr. Solomon Grace in particular! You forget I'm a stranger myself. I'm not annexed to your State.'

Solomon admitted this, but said it was an oversight in the 'Constitootion.'

'Now this,' said she, ' is why rejected suitors are not welcome to prudent women and good wives. They must run down the man we have chosen, and behind his back, too, nine times out of ten.'

'I'm darned if it isn't mean—as mean as dirt.'

This concession seemed so creditable that she invited him to be her beau—as far as the market.

Solomon could not believe his good fortune. She laughed at him, and enlightened him : 'Give me a fair excuse, do you think I

wouldn't rather have a decent man beside
me than take my walks alone? What a bad
opinion you must have of woman's sense! I
do suppose that gentleman you are named
after knew 'em better. To be sure, he had
six hundred teachers, poor man!'

'I would give his lot for my one.'

'Solomon,' said Mrs. Haynes, severely,
'flattery is poison, so come on. I won't stand
still to be poisoned.' So she went shopping,
and continued at it long after she had parted
with Solomon Grace.

Mrs. Mansell wandered on and on, and
then back, to and fro, Lucy prattling gaily,
and almost irritating her, until she turned
hungry. Then her mother bought her a piece
of pie with the only coin in her pocket, but
could not eat herself. Night fell, the lamps
were lighted; foot-sore, weary, and sick at
heart, she could hardly draw her limbs along,
and began to ask herself bitterly what she had
done to be abandoned again and again by

everybody. But in truth she was not abandoned by all; a wise and just Providence was
guiding her every step. At last she stopped
in despair, and began to speak her mind to
Lucy, since there was no one else :

' It is inconsiderate, it is cruel,' said she,
' and me a stranger in this great city. Why
couldn't he take me up with him to look for
lodgings? Oh, Lucy, my mind misgives me.'

' Sit down on those steps, mamma,' said
Lucy, with pretty affection.

' Indeed, I shall be glad to rest a bit.'

She sat down on the door-steps, and thoughts
tormented her she could not utter to Lucy.
This must be their old enemy, Drink. He
had looked so pale and exhausted. Oh, if it
was! Misery! for the habit once resumed,
after so long abstinence, would never be got
rid of. Here was a miserable prospect, and
in a foreign land as well: no friends to curb
him or stand by her. And then if he got
drunk he would be robbed. How lucky she
had sewed up the notes in his waistcoat! The

money! Another chill thought went through her like an ice-bolt. Why had she parted with it? She had been warned that whilst she held it she held her husband. It was but a momentary horror. She dismissed that suspicion as unworthy and monstrous, and was ashamed of herself for harbouring so base a fear.

Lucy saw the change in her distressed face, and came to a simple, comprehensive conclusion: 'Mamma, he is a wicked man.'

Sarah was shocked at this from her. 'No, no, my child; he is a good man, and your father.'

'Then fathers don't love us like uncles do. Uncle Joe would never have left us like this. I wish I had never left home.'

Sarah would not say that; but she sighed deeply, and rocked herself, country fashion, sitting on the stone steps.

Mrs. Haynes came back to her tea, and found her in that condition, while Lucy, standing beside her, opened two glorious eyes with

sorrowful amazement. For a moment Mrs.
Haynes thought they were beggars, but the
next her eye took in almost at one glance their
dress and neat appearance, and Lucy's ear-
rings, pearl and gold.

She asked Mrs. Mansell civilly what was
the matter—was she tired?

Mrs. Mansell looked up and said, sorrowfully, that she was in care and trouble. She
had lost her husband.

'What, dead?'

'Nay, Heaven forbid! But we parted on
the quay. He went to look for lodgings, and
he never came back. I don't know what to
think, nor what to do, I'm sure.'

'Dear me,' said the other; 'and you a
stranger in the country!'

Sarah sighed.

'And it is late for the child to be out.'

Sarah gave her a glance of maternal gratitude, and passed her arm round her child at
the very idea of any harm threatening her.

Mrs. Haynes looked well at them both, and

liked their faces even better than their appearance. She said good-naturedly: ' You had better step in and rest yourselves awhile, and then we'll see.'

' Thank you kindly, ma'am ; I'm sure it is very good of you.'

Mrs. Haynes opened the door with a latch-key and led the way to a back room of mixed character. There was a French bed in it with curtains descending from a circular frame. There was also a chest of drawers, and a sort of plate-chest on them ; a large easy chair, much worn ; and a round table, with a white cloth on it—in short, it was an unpretending snuggery.

' There, take off your bonnets and make yourselves comfortable,' said Mrs. Haynes. And while they were doing this, she whispered an order to her maid—her name was Millicent. Then she took cups and saucers out of a cupboard and wiped them herself ; and they talked all this while, she and Mrs. Mansell.

A housekeeper's vanity is always on the alert the moment a possible rival comes ; so,

as Mrs. Mansell looked like a person with a
house of her own, Mrs. Haynes said : 'You
musn't go by this room ; mine is a beautiful
house, but I take lodgers, and it is so full, that
I have to pig anywhere. It doesn't matter
much, you know, when one's husband is away.'

Lucy listened, and informed her mother,
with some surprise, that the young lady was
married.

'Why, bless the child, I have been married
twice. The first was an Illinois man. Ah! he
was a husband! This time it is Matthew
Haynes, an Englishman. I can't show him
you, for he has gone home to draw a legacy,
and that takes time.' She paused a moment to
pour out the tea.

'Are you a New York lady, if you please?'
enquired Sarah.

Mrs. Haynes poising the tea-pot in the air,
smiled at her simplicity. 'No,' said she. 'Are
you? Why, we both speak country English
as broad as a barn door. Bless your heart, I
knew you for a countrywoman the moment

you opened your mouth, and I shouldn't be
surprised if we came from the very same part.
I be Wiltshire.'

'And I'm Barkshire born and bred.'

'Didn't I tell 'ee?'

Here Millicent came in with a large dish of
fried oysters.

'You don't get such oysters as these in Barkshire, let me tell ye.'

'That we don't. I never saw so many all
at one time.'

The hostess helped them liberally, and the
wanderers enjoyed them to the full, and their
eyes brightened, and the colour came back to
their faces, and when, like a true wife, Mrs.
Haynes said, 'Now tell me about yours,' Mrs.
Mansell was more communicative than she
would have been to an older acquaintance.

'Oh, my man is an excellent husband. Indeed, he hasn't a fault that I know of, except
he takes a drop now and then.'

'Oh, they all do that at odd times,' said
the other, carelessly.

'And even that he has given up,' said Sarah, earnestly. ' Only he was so ill at sea and exhausted like. How else to account for his behaviour, I can't think ; and you know they are sometimes obliged to take a glass medicinal.'

' Ay, that is their chat; and 'tis the only medicine where one glass leads to another. There, don't you begin to fret again. You'll see yours long before I shall see mine.' Then she observed that Lucy could not keep her eyes open. So she went farther than she had intended at first ; she determined to let them sleep in the house. ' Take your bonnets,' said she, ' and come with me.' She opened one of two folding-doors, and showed them into a larger parlour, with a bachelor's bed in it. The carpet was up, and stood in a roll, but everything was clean. ' There, this room is let, but not till twelve to-morrow; you must excuse disorder. You put the little love to bed, and then we will have our chat out. Ah,' said she, with a sudden change of manner that

was sweet and touching, 'I had a little girl by
my first husband; she would be about the age
of yours if I could have kept her alive; so my
heart warmed to yours the moment I saw her
standing beside you on my step, and her young
eyes full of love and trouble.'

Mrs. Haynes cried a little at this picture
and her own sad reminiscences, and the happy
mother kissed the sorrowful one, and she kissed
her in return. Then Mrs. Haynes withdrew
and summoned her maid, and she cleared away
the things, and then they cleaned the cups and
saucers and had a gossip, for Mrs. Haynes
must have somebody to talk to. She was well
educated, not like Deborah Smart: for all that,
she never read a book now, and those who
won't read must talk.

The folding-doors were thin, and did not
meet very close; the new wood had shrunk:
and Sarah, without intending it, heard a word
every now and then, but she paid no attention.
The first thing the careful mother did was to

M

thrust her hand and arm all down the bed inside; and she instantly resolved not to put her girl into it. She told her she should not undress her. So Lucy knelt at her knee, and said her prayers. When she had done, she asked if she might pray for the good lady.

'Ay, do, dear, and so shall I. It's all we can do for her.' She pulled down the counter-pane, laid Lucy on the blanket, and put a shawl over her. All this time she was thinking, and now her thoughts found vent. 'My girl, is it not strange that those who are sworn to stay by us, and we by them, should fail us, and that a lady who never saw our faces before should open her arms and her house to us, because we are strangers in a foreign land? God bless her!'

There was a loud knock at the street-door. It was followed by an eager exclamation from the other room: 'Oh, Milly! Why, sure that's my husband's knock.'

'Oh! I hope it is,' cried Sarah, as Millicent and her mistress dashed into the passage.

There was a moment of suspense, and then joyful exclamations in the passage.

'It *is*, Lucy ; I am so glad,' Sarah cried.

'So am I, mamma.'

'This way! this way!' screamed Mrs. Haynes, pulling what seemed to Sarah to be rather an undemonstrative husband into her little room. 'I must have him all to myself.' Then there was a long and warm embrace.

Sarah was somehow conscious of what was going on. She sat down by Lucy, and said, a little sadly, 'Ay, they are happy, those two.' Then, cheerfully, 'Well, my turn *must* come.'

Sarah Mansell did not hear exactly what was said next, but I will tell the reader.

Mrs. Haynes, who had now turned the gas up, was concerned at her husband's appearance. 'La!' said she, 'how pale you look! Sit down in your own chair. (He staggered a little, but got into the chair all right.) 'I'll make you a cup of tea.'

'Tea be blowed!' said he, roughly.

Sarah heard that where she sat, with her

cheek against Lucy's. She started away from her, half puzzled, half amazed.

'Gimme — drop brandy,' said the man, louder still.

Sarah bounded with one movement into the middle of the room, and then stood panting. Even Lucy raised herself on her hands in the bed, and her eyes opened wide.

'I doubt you have had enough of that already,' was the reply in the next room. 'Why, now I think of it, you must have come by the steamboat eight hours ago. How many have you liquored with before your wife's turn came?'

'I don't know,' said he, like a dog's bark, loud and sharp and sullen.

Lucy heard, and slipped off the bed to her mother, full of curiosity. 'Why, mamma,' said she, ' that's——'

Before she could say the word, Sarah closed the child's mouth with her hand almost fiercely; then held her tight, and pressed the now terrified girl's face against her own body.

All the woman's senses were so excited that she heard through the doors as if they had been paper. And this is what she heard this man say, who was her husband and the husband of the woman that had sheltered her.

'If you *must* know, I was faint, and troubled in my mind, and just took one glass to keep my heart up and clear my head, and then one led to another. Never you mind. I'm a good husband to *you*, the best in England—no, the best in New York—the best in all the world; d'ye hear?'

'Yes,' said the other wife, 'I hear the good news; but please don't bawl it so loud.' Then she whispered something.

Sarah caught her girl up like a baby, was at the bed in a moment, laid her on it, and dared her to move with such a look and such a commanding gesture as the girl had never seen before. Then hissing out, 'I'll know all if it kills me,' she glided back like a serpent to the door. She put her ear to the very aperture.

Matthew Haynes, *alias* James Mansell, lowered his voice. 'You don't know the sacrifice, curse it all. One drop of brandy, for mercy's sake.'

'Only one, then.' She gave him a glass. He gulped it down.

'Ah!—It is no use snivelling ; I didn't mean to do it this way. But it was sure to come to this. I was in a cleft stick.'

'Whatever is the man maundering about?' said Elizabeth. 'Oh, cursed liquor!'

The moment she raised her voice, he raised his. 'D'ye want to wrangle? It isn't for you to grumble! *You* are all right. I'VE GOT THE FOUR HUNDRED POUNDS I WIRED YOU ABOUT!'

He uttered these words, not loudly, but very impressively, syllable by syllable.

And syllable by syllable they seemed to enter Sarah Mansell's body like javelins made of ice. The poor creature shrank altogether at first, and then slowly stretched herself out. Her arms strangely contorted themselves in agony, but at last spread feebly out, and her hands clutched vaguely, as if she was on a real cross, as well as on a cross of mental anguish; and when, after a few words of explanation, that told her nothing more, the other woman said, ' Well, you are a good husband; I must kiss you,' the limp body and drooping head of the true wife sank helpless against the door with a strange sound; it was gentle, yet heavy and corpse-like.

CHAPTER IX.

DOUBLEFACE, like others who have crime in hand, was startled by a sound the meaning of which he did not know. He thrust away his partner, and held her at arm's-length. 'What is that?' said he.

'Only my lodger,' said Elizabeth. 'I'll go and see what she wants.'

She stepped toward the door, against which Sarah was lying erect (I can describe it no other way), not insensible, but utterly limp and powerless to move, and indeed conscious that if she moved, she must fall headlong. At this crisis Doubleface turned jealous all of a sudden.

'No,' said he; 'bother your lodgers! I'm the master. Attend to me first. Here, help me off with my coat and waistcoat.'

' Now give me my dressing-gown.'

' Now my shoes.'

At last he rolled into bed. Now Elizabeth Haynes suspected her lodger of listening, and she thought it was too bad. She resolved to catch her.

She took off her shoes and stole on tiptoe from the bed to the door. At the same moment, Sarah Mansell, having nothing more to learn, made an effort to escape from her post of agony. She laid a hand on the projection of the door, and tottered a little way; from that to a chair which she clutched, and just as Elizabeth Haynes turned the door-handle she sank down by the bed, and seizing the clothes convulsively, she sank on her knees with her arms helpless before her, as the door opened and Mrs. Haynes peeped in. Then that lady thought she was praying, and postponed her examination until the morning.

She was not so far wrong; for the first thing the betrayed wife did, when she had power, was to pray over her fatherless child. She prayed to God for hours, and I think He heard her. It did not appear so at first. In that horrible night she lived a life of agony. She thought of all she had done and suffered for that man, and she was the milch cow, and on the other side that door was the wife.

Three thousand miles from home—a deserted wife. If ever a woman lived a year of torture in a night, she did. It exhausted her body so that she actually fell asleep for half an hour.

She dreamed the events of years; but at last her ever-changing dream culminated in a vision. She saw before her her own little parlour. In it sat Deborah and Pinder looking at a picture. The picture had no features to her, but Deborah's face and Pinder's were quite clear, and beautiful with affection. They said it was *her* picture, as beautiful as herself, and they feared they should never see her again. She dreamed she wanted to comfort them, and say 'You shall—you shall,' but her tongue was tied. The two faces then became angelic with affection, and vanished.

She awoke. She came back by degrees to her own misery. But how is this? The anguish that was so keen remains, but no longer pierces, stuns, galls, and maddens. It is blunted, and her heart seems turned to stone.

'Villain—drunkard—thief and traitor,' said she to herself. 'All this time everybody knew him but me. I've shed my last tear for him. I've turned against him. I'm a stone.'

She turned up the gas, and looked at Lucy. This moment she became conscious, then, that Lucy had no longer a rival in her heart.

She resolved to leave the place at once.

Suddenly she remembered the money Doubleface got out of her to make Lucy's fortune, as he said. She stooped over Lucy and kissed her, too softly to wake her. 'No, my fatherless girl,' said she, 'money is nothing to me now, but they sha'n't rob *you*. You shall have your own, if they kill me.'

She sat down quietly, and thought what was the best way to execute the design she had conceived in a moment; and not every one of us would have hit upon the right order of action so well. She began by doing in her own room all that could be done there at all. She put a small table near the gaslight, laid her scissors on it, threaded a needle, and fastened it to her sleeve.

Then she went softly, opened one of the folding-doors, and satisfied herself that Double-face and his other wife were asleep. Then she slipped into their room and turned up their gas a very little, found his trousers and his waistcoat under them, took away the waistcoat to her own room, and left the door ajar.

She brought the waistcoat to her table, cut the stitches, drew them away, took out the bank notes, and put them in her bosom, all as coolly as possible.

Then she sat quietly down and sewed up the top of the pocket again, imitating the very number of the stitches she had originally put in.

Then she took the waistcoat, went into the next room, and put it back on the chair exactly where she had found it, and laid the trousers on it.

Then, having resumed her own, and no longer caring so very much whether she was caught or not by a man whom she could send to prison for bigamy, she actually drew the curtain back a little, and folding her arms, surveyed the couple steadily with such an expression as seldom looks out of mortal eye. The husband lay on his back snoring loud, as he always did after excess. The other woman he had deceived lay on her side as innocent as a child, and sleeping like one.

The resolute woman who looked on stood there to be cured or die. Her flesh crawled and quivered at first, but she stood and clinched her teeth, and deliberately burned this sight into her heart, that she might never forget it, nor, by forgetting, be induced to forgive it.

Soon the day dawned, and a servant unbolted the street door.

Then Sarah made Lucy get up in silence, both put on their bonnets, and she took the little girl through the other room, keeping her on her other side, so that she could see nothing and walked out of the house without a word.

Late in the morning James Mansell awoke from a heavy sleep, and found himself alone in bed. He soon realised the situation drink had blunted overnight, and it frightened him. His thoughts were bitter. How drink had foiled all his cunning!

He had settled in his sober mind to play both women with consummate skill; not to go near Elizabeth in New York till he had settled Sarah in Boston, and stayed with her a month at least. What was to be done now? Why, snatch a mouthful, and then hunt after Sarah and tell her some lie, and fly with her to Boston, and write Elizabeth another lie to account for his departure.

He burst through the folding-doors, and threw them both wide open for air. In the room his haggard face looked into sat Elizabeth, smiling and making his tea, and getting break-

fast ready for him; her quick ear had heard
him move in the bedroom.

'That's right,' said he; 'give me a morsel
to eat. I must be off to the docks directly for
my luggage.'

'What, is your money and all at the
docks?'

'Not likely. That never leaves me night
and day.'

'La! then you might show it to me,' said
she.

'Perhaps you don't believe I have got it,'
said he.

'The idea! Of course I believe your word.'
She filled him a cup of tea, and said no more.
It was he who returned to the subject.

'Come, now, you'd like to see it, and make
sure?'

'Why, Matthew,' said she, 'what woman
wouldn't that had heard so much about it?'

'Here goes, then,' said he, and took off his
coat.

'What, in your coat?' said she. 'Oh

dear! That is not a very safe place, I am
sure.'

'Guess again,' said he. Then he opened
his waistcoat, and showed her the inside
pocket.

She peered across the table at it, and
approved.

'I see,' said she. 'Who'd have thought a
man had so much sense?' On reflection, however, she was not so pleased. 'Who sewed it in
for you?' said she, sharply. 'I can see the
stitches from here. 'Twas a woman.'

'Well, then, let a woman unsew it,' was
all the reply he deigned; and he chucked her
the waistcoat, and went on with his breakfast
very fast.

She took the waistcoat on her knee,
whipped her scissors out of her pocket, and
carefully snipped the stitches; then opened
the pocket, and groped in it with her fingers;
'Well, but,' said she, 'there's no money
here.'

'Gammon,' said he, with his mouth full.

She groped it thoroughly. 'But I say there isn't,' said she.

'Don't tell lies. Give it me.'

She gave it him and watched him keenly, and even suspiciously.

He felt the pocket—groped it—clutched it—turned it inside out : there was nothing.

'What in heaven is this?' he gasped. 'Am I mad? Am I dreaming? It is impossible. Cut the thing to pieces! Tear it to atoms! Robbed! robbed! I'll go for the police! I'll search every woman in the house.' And he started wildly up.

'But Elizabeth rose too, and said, very firmly: 'You'll do nothing of the kind ; there are no thieves here. Now sit down and think.'

'I can't ; I'm all in a whirl.'

'You must. Tell me the name of all the bars you drank at before you came here.'

He groaned, and mentioned several.

'Were there any women about?'

'Plenty at some of them.'

N

' Did you take your coat off? '

' Not likely.   I tell you I felt them in my pocket before I went to bed.'

' Ah! you thought so, perhaps.   Now who sewed them in for you? '

' No matter.'

' Who sewed them in for you ? '

' The tailor.'

' No, Matthew, a woman sewed them in; and a woman sewed the empty pocket up again this last time.   It is not a man's work, and, besides, men are not so artful as all that. There's more behind than you have told me,' and she fell into a brown study.

Doubleface took his resolution in a moment. He would go to the docks, wait there till Sarah came for her boxes, and tell her he had been set upon and robbed.   Then he would go away with her and work for a month, till she got more money from England.

So he told Elizabeth he would take the police to all those bars, and he went out hastily.

She made no objection; she sat there, and brooded over this strange mystery.

By-and-bye she had a visitor—an unexpected one, and one she could speak her mind to on this subject more openly than to her husband.

Sarah Mansell, on leaving that house, asked her way to the Custom-house. To her surprise it was very near. All her desire now was to get home. Her heart, always single, turned homeward entirely. Jealousy had tortured her too much. The torture that kills defeats itself, and her anguish had killed love as well as agonised it. And then she had her own special character; for women vary as men do: in some jealousy preponderates so that they cannot resign an unworthy man who belongs to them to another woman; in others jealousy, though terribly powerful, is curbed by pride and self-respect. These are the high-spirited women who will be the only one or none; and note this, the more they love a man the more

they will have him all to themselves, or part
with him root and branch : wild horses could
not tear them from that alternative. These
loving but resolute women belong to no class
in society, and are found in every class.
Books, journals, education, ignorance, neither
make nor mar them. It is a law of their
nature, though not the general law.

Sarah found that a steamboat started for
England that day. She instantly took a berth
for Lucy and herself, and meantime she took
her boxes away in a cab, lest James Mansell
should come and find them there, and wait
about for her. She did not fear him one bit;
but she abhorred the sight of him now.

She directed a carman to drive her to any
good hotel he chose, only let it be a mile
distant.

James Mansell came to the Custom-house,
inquired for her boxes, and found that his wife
had removed them and gone to a hotel. The
carman who took her had not returned, but a
person James feed promised to ask him on his

return to what hotel he had driven the lady. Then Mansell went back to get some money from Elizabeth; for he had drunk all his loose cash the day before.

The visitor she received meantime was Solomon Grace. He came in rather sheepishly, and began to plead her permission, but she cut all that short very brusquely.

'You come at the right time. I have been robbed of 400*l*.'

Then she told him all that had passed between her and Matthew, and Solomon offered his theory, videlicet, that the notes had never existed.

'Well, then, I think they did,' said Elizabeth. 'But here's my trouble. There's a person I suspect; but I don't like to tell *him*; he might blame me for housing a stranger, and indeed it was a foolish thing of me—there!—I gave a night's lodging to an Englishwoman and her child. She said she had come by the boat, and lost her husband. I am afraid she

never had one.　Anyway, she slept here in
this very room, and, Solomon, whilst my man
was telling me in there he had got me the
400*l.*, she came bounce against that door, and
I thought at the time she was listening.'

'She is the one that did the trick,' was
Solomon's conclusion.

However, to make sure, he asked if Mr.
Haynes had told her where the notes were
while the woman was listening.

'He must have,' said Elizabeth.　Then she
thought a bit.　'Why, la, no, he didn't.　She
could hear no more than I did, and certainly I
didn't know, nor he didn't tell me until this
morning, breakfast-time.　There—she couldn't
know—unless she had sewn them in, and that's
against all reason.　It's a mystery; it is quite
beyond me.'

Solomon puzzled over it in turn.　He said
there was a good-looking woman sat waiting
for her husband best part of two hours at the
Custom-house, and a child with her.

'A girl?'

' Yes, a girl.'

' What had she on? '

' Didn't observe.'

' What was the child like? '

' Darkish—beautiful black eyes—a picture!'

' That is them, I shouldn't wonder. You saw no husband, I'll go bail.'

' Ay, but I did—saw his back, however. That one is no thief—a plain, honest woman, with a face something between a calf and an angel.' ·

' Indeed,' said Elizabeth, ' she looked honest; and if her tale was true, it seems hard to suspect her. But it is a puzzle.'

Then Solomon Grace summed up the evidence: ' He drinks and gambles. One of those ways is enough. Such a man is soon eased of 400*l.* in New York city. I've seen a many drained out here with dice and drink, but I never knew a fool's pocket picked of notes sewn into the lining. Puzzle or not, that's a lie, I swan.'

The latter part of this summing up was

heard by Mr. Mansell from the parlour, he having slipped into the house the back way. He came in lowering, and put in his word. ' Did you ever know an honest man slip into a house and backbite a man to his wife ? '

Solomon turned red with ire and shame, for his position was not a perfect one. ' Can't say ever I did, but I've known folk the truth was pison to wherever told.'

' And the truth is that you are a discarded lover of my wife's, and a mischief-making hypocrite.'

Elizabeth was alarmed, for she knew Solomon could wring this bantam's neck in a moment, and she had no blind confidence in his pacific disposition, though he vaunted it so highly. ' La! Matthew, do you want every bone in your skin broken ?   And, Solomon, you must excuse him for my sake ; he is in great trouble.   I won't detain you at present.'

' That means make tracks,' said poor Solomon. ' I'm pacific,' said he, almost crying with vexation. ' I'll go sartain. I'd better go. But, Britisher—'

' Well, what is it, old Ohio ? '

' A word at parting.'

' In Chicageese ? '

' " Every dog has his day." That's English, I rather think.'

When he was gone, Elizabeth took a cheerful tone. She told James she did not for one moment believe he had drunk or gambled away 400*l.* ' But,' said she, ' it is no use being angry with Solomon Grace for saying what all the world says.' Then after a little while she played the philosopher. ' If you gave me my choice, and said, " Will you have 400*l.* or a sober, industrious husband ? " do you think I'd choose the money ? Never. So don't let us cry over spilt milk, but just you drop gambling—you don't drink as you used—and we shall do first-rate. The house is full, and all the lodgers like me. It always will be full now. Starting

was the only trouble.   I will undertake to keep
you if you will only spend your evenings with
me.'

James Mansell pretended to jump at these
terms, and Elizabeth invited him to go out
walking with her in an hour's time.

He agreed with feigned alacrity, and she
dressed for the occasion, and they walked out
arm in arm, she gay as a lark, he moody and
distracted, and attending to her flow of talk only
by fits and starts.

Meanwhile Mrs. Mansell and Lucy had a
nice wash and a good breakfast, and by-and-by
a conveyance was at the door to take their
boxes to the boat.

But Lucy was most unwilling.   'Oh,
mamma,' she said, ' we have only just come.'

' I can't help that,' was the dogged reply.

'But everything is so beautiful, and the
people so kind : they call me " miss" ! '

'My child,' said her mother, 'I must go
home.   Wounded creatures all go home ; and

I am wounded to the heart. I have nobody now but you : be kind to me.'

Lucy flung her arms round her mother's neck. 'Oh, mamma, I'll go with you to Jericho.'

CHAPTER X.

IT seemed as if everything was to be smoothed for their going home.   At the docks they found Solomon Grace superintending Custom-house work, and Sarah beckoned him, and asked him how she should get her boxes on board.

'Going home already?   What, without your husband?'

'Sir, my husband has abandoned me.'

'What, altogether?'

'Me and my child.'

'The miserable cuss.'

Having thus delivered himself, he said it was his business to obey her orders.   He couldn't leave that spot just then, but if she would give him the ticket, his mate should stow her things in the cabin.   This was done accordingly.   Meantime he asked leave to put her a question.

'As many as you please,' said she, calmly.

'Where did you sleep last night?'

'With a lady who called herself Mrs. Haynes.'

'At One-hundred-and-fourth Street?'

'I don't know, unfortunately. But since you ask, perhaps you know that Mrs. Haynes.'

'I rather think I do.'

'That is curious.'

'Well, no. I've known her nine years. Why, her first husband was a cousin of mine. When he died I always intended to be number two; only I didn't like to ask her in the church-yard; but that 'ere Britisher warn't so nice; he slipped in ahead of me.'

Sarah turned her brown eye full on him with growing interest. 'I understand perfectly,' said she. 'You respected her most because you loved her best.'

Solomon stared at her. He was utterly amazed, but at the same time charmed, at this gentle stranger reading him so favourably all in a moment, and reading him right. He asked

her a little sheepishly if he might make so free
as to take her hand. 'You are very welcome,
I am sure,' said she, smiling calmly.

'I'll tell *you* the truth,' said he, 'though it's
agin myself. I love her still; can't get her out
of my head nohow.'

'Why should you?' said she, loftily.

Solomon stared at that.

'It's like poor Joe Pinder,' said she, half to
herself.

'Can't say; don't know the family.'

Sarah began to wonder. Presently she
scanned him all over with her steady eyes: 'I
think,' said she, slowly, 'it must be my duty to
write a note to Mrs. Haynes.'

'About her housing you for the night?'

'About that and other things. You know
her and respect her; will you give it her?'

'Of course I will.'

'Into her own hand?'

'And glad of the job.'

'Not into the hands of the man.'

'What! her husband—the cuss—not likely.'

Satisfied on that point, Sarah said she would like to go on board out of the bustle. She could write the letter in the cabin ; it would be a short one. Then Solomon took her and Lucy on board. After some little preparation Sarah took paper and an envelope out of her bag : she had everything ready to write to her sister. She sat down and wrote to the other wife of James Mansell. Solomon Grace had nothing else to do but to watch her, and he did wonder what that thoughtful brow and white hand were sending to the woman he still loved.

It was no simple matter ; the Englishwoman had a difficult task before her. She paused at every line. Her face was solemn, grave, and powerful. So the puzzle deepened. Solomon could see this was not a woman writing merely to thank another for a night's lodging. When she had finished it, she folded it and secured it very carefully, and beckoned Solomon Grace.

He came to her.

'You will give this letter into her own hand, and see her read it ? '

'I will ; who shall I say it is from ? '

·'Sarah Mansell.'

'Oh ! Sarah Mansell.   You are Sarah Mansell ? '

'I am Sarah Mansell.'   Then she said, very
thoughtfully, ' This Mrs. Haynes, have you a
real affection for her ? '

'I am a bachelor for her sake, that is all,'
said he, despondently.

She fixed her eyes on him.   ' Perhaps some
day you may be a married man for her sake.'

Solomon   shook   his   head.   ' Is   that   a
conundrum ? '

' Well,' said she,' the future *is* a riddle.
What I am doing now proves that.   Who
knows?   You have been very kind to me.
Blessings come to those who are good to the
stranger, the fatherless, and the widow.   Well,
my child is fatherless this day, and I am a
deserted wife, all alone on the great sea, with
nobody but my child and my God.'

Poor Solomon might have told her those
two were more than seventy-seven bad hus-

bands, but she went too straight for the tender heart that lay beneath his breast.

'Don't ye now, don't ye,' he snivelled; 'you'll make me cry enough to wash a palace-car. You're not alone, you sha'n't be alone. Here, little beauty, come and comfort mother. Solomon Grace isn't much, but he'll stand by you till she starts, and then you must just keep your eye square for home, like the jade's figure-head there. You have got friends to home?'

'I have.'

'You are loved to home?'

'I am, sir.'

'Don't I tell you. They're waiting for you; they are thinking of you.'

'They are. I saw them in a vision last night.'

'It stands to reason; you was born to be loved.'

'I thought so once, sir.'

'I think so now, and I'm sure of it. You'd bewitch creation. Why, I'd cut myself in pieces to serve you. Darn me if I wouldn't

o

take you safe to that ar island and hand you to
your friends, and then slip back, if it warn't
for the letter.'

Leaving this good soul to comfort Sarah
Mansell till the ship was cleared of strangers, I
must go to meet a less interesting couple, who
are coming this way.

As James took the walk merely to please
Elizabeth, he went wherever she chose. They
called at a provision shop and bought the things
he liked. Elizabeth was handsome and well
dressed, and many admiring glances were cast
on her. Her companion's vanity was tickled
at this. Only what rather spoiled the walk
was that he longed so at that very moment to
be raking the town for the other.

Presently they came out in sight of the
quay, and James began to fidget again. He
burned to get away from his companion to see
if his agent had news of Sarah, and, besides
that, he had a dread of open spaces—they
facilitate surprises. Sarah might see him from

a distance walking with Elizabeth. This ex-
treme uneasiness did not escape the latter.
'Why, what is the matter with you now?' said
she. 'You keep looking about as if you had
done something, and expected the police to
pounce on you from every corner.'

'You wouldn't be easy if you had lost
400*l.*, and couldn't tell how.'

'Yes, I would, if I could do without them.
They were for *me*, but I don't fret, and why
waste another thought on them, my dear?'

At this moment the steamer's bell rang.
'There, now,' said Elizabeth, kindly, 'stay and
see the boat start.'

'Lend me a couple of dollars,' said he. She
gave it him directly. 'Wait a bit for me here,'
he said, and Elizabeth seated herself in a sort
of pleasant waiting-room near the main entrance
to the piers, and waited.

He darted into a shop and replenished his
flask. Then he ran to find his agent, and got
from him the name of the hotel Sarah Mansell
had gone to. He was eager to go there at

once, but dared not. Elizabeth had a temper. Doubleface was fairly puzzled between the two. However, it was only postponed for an hour. Elizabeth, with her house full of lodgers, would not be out more than that, and then he would fly on the wings of penitence to Sarah, and not leave her for the other till he had humbugged her thoroughly and eradicated all suspicion.

So he came back to Elizabeth. She was sitting there quite at ease. ' Curse it,' said he, ' she must go home.'

But now ropes were cast off, and every preparation made for the vessel leaving. This is admirably managed in New York. The largest steamboat just glides away into the Atlantic like a river-boat starting upon the Thames.

' Ah,' said Doubleface, tormented by the situation he had created for himself, ' I wish I was going in you—alone.' He stepped forward and saw her move away. She lay against the quay amidships, but she was so long that it took a minute before her after-cabin came opposite.

A woman, who had caught sight of James

Mansell, but hidden herself till then, rushed out upon the poop, followed by a girl. She whipped a packet of notes out of her bosom, and brandished them high in the air to him, then drew her child's head to her waist.

That is what she did. But how can words convey the grandeur of those impassioned gestures, the swiftness of their sequence, and the tale that towering figure and those flaming eyes told to the villain and fool who had possessed her, plagued her for years, and hit upon the only way to lose her.

He started back, bewildered, blasted, terrified, and glared after her in stupid dismay.

While he stood petrified, a voice hissed in his ear, 'You know—where—your—notes—are—now!'

It was Elizabeth at his shoulder, but a little behind him. Doubleface turned slowly, aghast with this new danger. He gasped, but could not articulate.

Elizabeth laid her right hand on his shoulder, and pointed to Sarah with her left.

'Why, that woman is shaking them in your face!' Then she took him by both shoulders and turned him square to her. 'Your face, that is as white as ashes!' In this position she drove her eyes into his, and clutched him firmly. 'What is there between that woman and you? She has taken your money, yet she is not afraid. She vaunts it, and it's you that tremble. Oh! what does this mean?'

In her excitement she had grasped him so firmly that her nails hurt him severely through his clothes, out now that clutch relaxed, and she felt weak. 'What does this mean?' she repeated.

The other creature, accustomed to lie, now tried to escape, hopeless as it seemed. He stammered: 'I don't know. I saw a woman shake something or other at me—was it at me?'

'Who else?'

'I fancied she looked past me somehow. Where were you?'

'Behind you at the door.'

'Could it be to you?' The desperate wretch hardly knew what he was saying. To his surprise this bold suggestion told.

'Why, of course it *might* be to me.'

He seized this advantage artfully. 'More likely to neither of us,' said he; 'and yet I don't know; since I came home everything that happens is a mystery.'

'That is true, and I suppose I shall never know the meaning of it all.'

'I'm as much in the dark as you are,' said he, 'and you can believe me or not, as you like.' Then he took a step or two away to show her he was disposed to quarrel with her. That answers sometimes when a body is in the wrong.

This stroke of policy left room for a third figure to step in between them, and that position was promptly taken by Solomon Grace.

'Letter from Sarah Mansell.'

Doubleface turned with a yell, and made a grab at the letter. Solomon, who was holding it out with his right hand toward Elizabeth, stopped the rush with his left, and mocked the attempt. 'No, yer don't,' said the stalwart giant : 'I'm under Mrs. Sarah Mansell's orders as this letter is not to be intercepted by any darned cuss whatever, but guv into the hands of Mrs. Haynes, and read before me to make sure.'

Elizabeth stared, but hesitated to defy her husband before Solomon Grace. 'But I don't know her,' said she, looking at the letter in Solomon's hand.

'Yes, ye do—it's the lady that slept at your house last night.'

Elizabeth uttered a little cry and panted. She almost snatched the letter now, and said, 'Then she did listen at the door.'

'Like enough,' said James. 'Then of course she'll know what to say to set us all by the ears.'

'Yes, but,' said Elizabeth, 'she knows more than you ever told me that night. She knew where to find those notes—ay, those that hide can find. My fingers tremble ; open it for me, Solomon.'

He opened the letter, and handed it to Elizabeth, and dared James Mansell to interfere. Elizabeth read the letter very slowly, and piecemeal—read it how she could indeed ; for her turn was come to have her bosom pierced :

' " MADAM,—You and I—are both unfortunate. You are betrayed, and I am deceived. If I tell the truth, I must pain you ; if I withhold it, he will deceive you still." Oh, what is coming?' said poor Elizabeth. " The man that passes for Matthew Haynes " '—she stopped and looked at him, and read again—' " passes for Matthew Haynes—is James Mansell—my husband ! " ' (the reader held out her hand piteously to Solomon Grace ; he supported her, and she held on to him, and that seemed to give her more power to read on) ' " We were married at St. Mary's Church, Glo'ster, on the 13th of July, 1873.' "

' That's a lie,' said James.

' It does not read like one,' was the dogged reply.

' " In 1878 he robbed me of my savings, and went to America. Last month one Varney from Liverpool told him I had money. He came for it directly, and took me with it—it was 400*l.*—sooner than not have it at all. Dear madam, I could not let my child be robbed." There, I knew it—she took back her own. " But James Mansell is yours if worth keeping." Are you worth keeping?   " My door he never enters again.   But if ever *you* should be as desolate as I was on your steps that bitter night, my home is yours.   God help us both !

"SARAH MANSELL,

" 13 Green Street, Liverpool." '

' That is as clever a lie as ever woman told,' said James Mansell.

Elizabeth replied : ' It is God's truth! Sunshine is not clearer. So, then, I never had but one husband.' She put both hands to her face and blushed to the throat. 'You were his friend. Take me home.' She clung piteously to Solomon. Then she turned to Doubleface. 'In one hour my servant will give you your clothes on my door-step. My door you never enter again.'

'Mind that!' said the Illinois man. 'I shall be there. "Every dog has his day!"' With the word he tucked the resolute but trembling Elizabeth tight under his arm and took her home.

Doubleface cursed them both as they retreated. Then he rushed to the water-side, and the steamboat was now all in sight, and Sarah Mansell still visible, standing over her child with her eyes raised to heaven.

Then the fool and villain raged and raved between the two superior women he had deceived and lost. Both too good for him, and at last he knew it—both in sight, yet leaving him for ever, and he knew it. He raved; he cursed; he ran to the water's edge. No, he had not the courage to die. He took out his flask and went for comfort to his ruin—he drank neat brandy fiercely.

Then fire ran through his veins. He began not to care quite so much. He drank again. Aha! He was brave. He defied them. He drank both their healths in brandy. He vowed to have two more as good as either of them. He drank on till his eyes set and he rolled upon the pavement. There the police found him dead drunk, and held a short consultation over him.

' Police cell? '

' No—hospital.'

CHAPTER XI.

Joseph Pinder and Deborah Smart kept the home and the little shop, and were on those terms of gentle fellowship which often lead to a closer union when some stronger attachment ceases to interfere. When a month had elapsed they began to be very anxious to hear from Sarah; and one evening Pinder said if she had written the day she landed, or even the day after, they ought to have had a letter that very day.

'Oh!' said Deborah, 'he won't let her write to *us*. That is my trouble now—we shall never know whether she is dead or alive.'

Pinder could not bring himself to believe that; so then they had a discussion. It was interrupted by the rattle of a fly drawing up at the door Wheel visitors were rare at that

house.   Deborah thought the man had drawn
up at the wrong door ; Pinder said he would
go and see ; a knock at the door settled the
question   Pinder opened it ; and there, full in
the gas-light, stood Sarah Mansell and Lucy.
Pinder uttered a loud exclamation.   She gave
a little sign of satisfaction, and put both hands
on his shoulders.   ' Yes, my good Joseph, here
we are, thank Heaven !   Oh, sister ! ' and she
stopped Deborah's scream of amazement and
delight by flying into her arms.   The cab was
paid, the boxes taken into the parlour, and
then Sarah and Lucy were inspected and
cuddled again.

 Then came a fusillade of questions.   ' But
what brought you back so soon?   Did he
change his mind ?   I never thought he would
let you come back at all.   And looking like a
rose ; you are properly sunburned ; but it
becomes you—everything becomes my sister.
Here's your picture ; it has been our only comfort.   Aren't you hungry after your journey ? '
    ' Indeed I am.'

'Bless you! And I could almost bless him
for bringing you back in such health and
spirits. There, you go upstairs and make
yourselves comfortable; your supper shall be
ready in ten minutes. Oh dear! I don't know
whether I'm on my head or my heels for
joy.'

In due course the cloth was laid for five,
and supper served.

'Will he be here to supper?' asked Deborah,
with a laughable diminution of ardour.

'No.'

'That is odd. Of course he will sleep
here?'

'No.'

At this Deborah and Pinder sat open-
mouthed, and could hardly believe their senses.
Sarah, brimful of health and in good spirits,
yet her husband not with her. He could not
be far off, thought Deborah.

'He is in Liverpool?'

'No.'

'Then he is coming by next boat?'

' No.'

' Well, I never.'

' Let us welcome her, not question her,' suggested Pinder; ' she will tell us all about it when she chooses. It is enough for me to see her looking so well and so happy.'

' Happy, because I am at peace, and because I have got back to two dear friends. Ah! I saw you both in my dream, sitting over that picture there and saying, " We shall never see her again."'

' O gracious heavens! and so we did,' cried Deborah.

' I was sure of it,' Sarah replied, ' the vision was so plain.'

Deborah's curiosity burned her; she could not help putting questions directly or indirectly. Sarah parried them calmly; then came a practical and somewhat delicate question. Deborah approached it indirectly:

' Since you went I was afraid to be alone in the house, and Mr. Pinder he has slept in Lucy's room.'

Sarah saw at once what she would be at, and said: 'Pray make no change for me. Lucy will sleep with me in the best bedroom. We shall both prefer it, shall we not?'

'Oh yes, mamma! I like to be with you day and night.'

Deborah was charmed at the arrangement, and so was Pinder; he had expected to be politely consigned to some other dwelling. Deborah, however, must try once more to draw her sister.

'This is a blessed state of things,' said she, 'but I am afraid 'tis too good to last. He will drop on us some day, and turn us to the right-about.'

Sarah would not utter a syllable in reply, and wore an impassive countenance, as she took no interest whatever in the speculation. It must be confessed this was enough to exasperate curiosity. 'Well,' said Deborah, in despair, 'will you answer me one thing? Has he collared the money?' Sarah put her hand to her bosom, and produced a bundle of notes.

P

'It is all here except the travelling expenses,' she said, calmly.

'I am glad of that,' said Pinder; 'and for pity's sake, don't question her any more.'

Sarah smiled. 'Don't be hard on her, Joseph,' said she. 'She must ask questions, being a woman, and one that loves me. But I'm not bound to answer them, you know.'

'If she won't bear to be questioned, she shall go to bed, for I am dying with curiosity. Aren't you, Mr. Pinder? Now tell the truth.'

'Well, I am,' was the frank reply. 'But I don't want to know everything all in a moment. I'd rather have her here and know nothing more than know everything and *not* have *her.*'

Deborah acquiesced hypocritically, because she had just remembered she could get it all out of Lucy. That young lady now showed fatigue, and the little party separated for the night.

'One word,' said Deborah to Sarah in her

bedroom. 'Give me one word to sleep on. Are you happy?'

'Sister, I am content.'

Deborah pumped Lucy. Lucy, to her infinite surprise, pursed up her lips, and would not say a word.

Her mother had made her promise most solemnly not to reveal anything whatever that had happened to them in New York.

Deborah writhed under this, but Pinder made light of it, and really there was plenty to balance the want of complete information. Sarah resumed her business; he was once more her associate, and his jealousy was set to sleep.

Her husband was not there, and no longer filled her thoughts. She never fretted for him; indeed, she ignored the man. The phenomenon was new and unaccountable, but certain. Joseph Pinder threw himself with more ardour than ever into her service, and persuaded her to seize an opportunity, and rent larger and better-situated premises in a good thoroughfare.

Here their trade was soon quadrupled, and
Sarah Mansell was literally on the road to
fortune. By-and-bye Lucy's health failed. It
was 'Pinder to the rescue' directly. He took
a little villa and garden outside the town, and
there he established Deborah and Lucy with a
maid-servant. Sarah slept there. Pinder had
a room there, but generally slept on the old
premises.

All this time he was making visible advances
in the affection of Sarah Mansell. Indeed, that
straightforward woman never condescended to
conceal her growing affection for him. The
change was visible on the very night of her
arrival, but now, as the months rolled on, her
innocent affection and tenderness for the friend
who had suffered for her and loved her these
ten years grew and grew. Deborah saw it.
Lucy saw it. The last to see it was Joseph
himself; but even he discovered it at last with
a little help from Deborah. In truth, it was
undisguised. The only mystery was how it
could be reconciled with her character, for she

was a wife, and the most prudent of women. Then why let Joseph Pinder see he was the man she cared for, and the only one? However, one day the exultant Joseph found there were limits. In the ardour of his affection he went to kiss her. She drew back directly: ' Please don't forget I am James Mansell's wife.' And for a day or two after that her manner was guarded and reserved. This was a warning to Mr. Joseph Pinder. A full and sweet affection visibly offered, but passion declined without a moment's hesitation. Joseph was chilled and disappointed for the moment, but what he had endured for her in less happy times reconciled him to the limits she now imposed. The situation was heavenly compared with those that had preceded it, and above all he saw nobody to be jealous of. He had also little auxiliary joys in the affection of Lucy and Deborah. These two, as well as Sarah, loved, petted, and made much of him.

How long this placid affection and sweet tranquil content—the most enduring happiness nature permits, if man could but see it—might have endured, I cannot say, for it was cut short about ten months after Sarah's return by a revelation that let in passion and let out peace.

They did now a brisk trade with the United States; and one evening a new agent came from New York with liberal offers. This man happened to be a gossip and a friend of Solomon Grace. '" Mansell!"' said he (the name over the shop). 'I could tell you a queer story connected with that name.'

'It's not an uncommon name,' said Pinder. 'Was it James Mansell?'

'No; it was a woman—a Mrs. Mansell. My friend Grace's wife—that is now—found her seated on a doorstep with a little girl; she said she had missed her husband. Mrs. Grace —at least, Mrs. Haynes, she was then—asked her in, and liked her so well she gave her her supper and a bed. Presently, home comes Mr. Haynes, her husband, quite unexpected. They had a hug or two, I suppose, and talked of their family affairs. And it seems this Mrs. Mansell listened, for next day this Haynes, as he called himself, missed 400*l.* sterling that was sewed inside his pocket. There was a row; one said one thing, one said another. Then— let me see—what's next? Oh, I remember!— what do you think? Mr. and Mrs. Haynes were watching the steamboat starting for England. Doesn't Mrs. Mansell step on deck all of a sudden and shakes the missing bank-notes in both their faces—'

'Capital!' roared Pinder. 'Go on! go on!'

'And it turned out she had only taken back her own, for this Haynes was no Haynes at all, but one Mansell, if you please, and had been taking a turn at bigamy.'

'The scoundrel! Now I see it all.'

'However, it didn't pay. Both the women sacked him, and Mrs. Haynes' friends wanted to imprison him. But Solomon Grace said, "Don't let's have a row. Marry me." Mind, he had always been sweet on her. So she married him like a bird. Why, you seem quite fluttered like. Do you know the people?'

'I do. This very shop belongs to that same Mrs. Mansell. Do tell! How things come about!'

'But of course the story is no news to you?' said the agent.

'Yes, it is. She never mentions his name.'

'No wonder. It must be a sore subject.'

'Where is the villain?' What has become of him? Any chance of his coming over here?'

'How can I tell?'

You may imagine the effect of this story upon Pinder. He went out to the villa hot with it, and glowing with love and pity for Sarah and rage at her husband. But during the walk he cooled a little, and began to ask himself if he ought to go and blurt out his information.

Sarah must have some reason for withholding it so long. Why, of course she was mortified, and would not thank him if he went and published it. Herein he misunderstood Sarah's motive—it was more profound, and the result of much thought and forecast. However, she will speak for herself. As for Pinder, he took a middle course: he confided it to Deborah, stipulating that she should feel her way with Sarah, and see how she could bear the truth being known.

Deborah acted on these instructions. But Sarah broke through them all in a moment, and told her the whole truth.

Next morning after breakfast she spoke privately to Pinder.

'So you have heard something about what parted James Mansell and me for ever?' (She had divined at once it must have come through Pinder.)

'Yes, Sarah, to tell the truth, I have.'

'Well, Deborah will tell you the whole story. It is not a matter I care to talk about.'

'I would rather have heard it from you than from a stranger. Did you doubt whose side I should be on?'

'No, Joseph, not for a moment. If you

must know, it was entirely for your sake I kept it to myself.'

'For my sake? Why, it only makes my heart warm a little more to you. To think that such an angel as you should ever be deceived and pillaged!'

'And cured. Believe it or not, I am thankful it happened, and almost grateful to the man for undeceiving me before I wasted any more affection on such a creature. No, Joseph. I am single-hearted, as I always was, and my heart turned to you before ever you saw my face this time, and I kept that cruel story locked in my bosom for your sake. Ah, well! I was not to have my way. You know my condition now—neither maid, wife, nor widow—and I am afraid it will unsettle your mind, and this will not be the happy home it has been.'

She sighed as she said this. He smiled at her wild apprehensions. But she was wise, and one that knew the heart of a man, and had forecasts.

CHAPTER XII.

THE only difference it made at first was a slight increase of sympathy and respect on the part of Joseph Pinder. But this was followed by a more manifest ardour of devotion, and this in due course by open courtship.

Sarah thought it due to herself and her position to curb this. She did so with admirable address, sometimes playfully, sometimes coldly, sometimes firmly, always kindly; yet with all this tact the repeated checks made Pinder cross now and then.

She was sorry, but out of prudence would not show it. It ended in his begging pardon, and in her saying she did not blame him; it was the natural consequence of her situation, now that situation was declared.

As nothing stands still, this went on till the

very thing Sarah had foreseen came to pass. The man after so many years of self-restraint, and so many good offices done, found himself at last rewarded with affection only. *That* was so sweet, that instead of satisfying him, it enticed him on ; he longed to possess her, and asked himself why not. It was no longer either wrong or impossible. He implored her to divorce James Mansell and marry him. She received the proposal with innocent horror. ' For shame ! ' she said—' oh,. for shame ! ' and turned her back on him, and would hardly speak to him for some hours.

He took the rebuff humbly enough at the time. But afterward he consulted his friends, and they sided with him, and he returned to the charge. He pressed her, he urged her, he coaxed her, he did everything except remind her of his own merits (and her own heart supplied that omission), but she would not yield. And the provoking thing was, she would not argue. Her old-fashioned religion and her old-fashioned delicacy despised reason-

ing on such a matter. He might almost
as well have offered her reasons for bigamy.
She was prejudiced and deaf to logic.
The next time he attacked her she showed
distress. 'Ah,' she said, 'I foresaw this.
Now you know why I kept my sad story
to myself. I know the value of peace and pure
affection, and I know that you or any man
would demand more than I can give. I don't
blame you, dear; but you will not forgive me;
it is not likely.' Her tears, the first he had
ever made her shed, melted him. He kissed
her, and begged her to forgive him. She
sighed and said, 'I suppose it is no use telling
you what it costs me to deny you. You will
never be easy now, but will never move *me*.
I can't help it. I must trust in God.'

Joseph Pinder told his friends it was no
use; he couldn't move her; he only tormented
himself and made her unhappy. Then one of
them laughed in his face, and told him he was
loving the woman like a calf and not like a
man. If she is really fond of you, be her

master. She'll like you all the better, whatever she may pretend. You cut it for a year or two, and let her find out what you are worth.

Another told him he was being humbugged and made a convenience of. The woman was secretly hoping her husband would come back and eat humble pie. So what with passion, the sense of long service, instilled distrust, and wounded vanity, Joseph Pinder, after disquieting himself and Sarah in vain for six months, resolved to *make a change.* One Saturday night he packed up his carpet-bag, and announced that he should go next morning to Manchester, and thence to London.

'For how long?' asked Sarah, anxiously.

'Well, Sarah, for good, unless something happens.'

Sarah said nothing; she understood in a moment that he intended to make a last attempt, and to go if she refused.

Next morning she went to church just as usual, and Joe Pinder awaited her return— with his ultimatum.

However, his feelings were subjected to some little trials before she came home.

It was a glorious day.

Lucy and Deborah sat out in the little garden. He finished packing his bag, and then went down to say a last word to them. He found Deborah with red eyes, and silent too — very unusual things with her. She and Lucy had evidently been talking the matter over, for Lucy asked him plump why her mother would not marry him. He replied, sullenly, ' Because I don't deserve it, you may be sure.'

' That is a fib,' said Lucy, severely. ' Well, if she won't, you had better marry me. Anything is better than being cross.'

' You must grow up first,' suggested Deborah.

' Or I must grow down,' said Pinder.

Then he took Lucy on his knee, and being in no humour for jest, he said : ' I had set my heart on you for a daughter. A wife I might find, but a daughter like you, all ready to love me—a regular rose-bud ! Ah, well !'

Lucy, precocious in all matters of sentiment, gushed out directly: 'You shall, you shall. Why, now I think of it, I want a father. I never much liked the other one. But I like you, Uncle Joe—I mean Father Joe. There, I love—I adore you.' She spread her arms supernaturally wide, and threw them round his neck with an enthusiastic rush.

'Little angel,' said the affectionate fellow. 'Well, Lucy, I'll try for you, but I suppose it is no use. Yes, Deborah,' said he, 'I'll go for my bag, and a few minutes will decide.'

Deborah could not blame him, for she knew that if she'd been a man, she could not have been so patient as Joe Pinder had been. There was a wicket-gate at the back of the garden, and Sarah now appeared at it. She had risen in the world. Both she and Deborah were dressed in rich black silk dresses, but with no trimming or flounces. Being tall, they showed off the material all the more. Sarah had a white French bonnet and neat gloves, but, relic of humility, she carried her prayer-book in her hand.

Deborah sent Lucy indoors, and went to meet her sister. ' Oh, Sarah,' she said, all in a hurry, ' do mind what you're about. Joe Pinder's blood is up. I think it is his friends that jeer him.'

Sarah sighed, ' What can I do ? '

' You can't do nothing, but you can say a deal. Why, what is a woman's tongue for? Tell him anything, promise anything. La! I wish I was in your place—he should never leave me.'

Before Sarah could answer, Pinder appeared at the door with a large carpet-bag. He put it down on the steps. Deborah ran to him.

' Oh, Joseph,' she said, pathetically, ' what should we do without thee ? And look at the garden—not a flower but you planted, and 'twas you laid the turf. Joe, dear, don't believe but she loves you with all her heart. She never could love two since she was born, and you are the *one*.'

' That remains to be seen,' said the man, firmly ; and he looked so pale and so dogged

Q

Deborah had little hope he would give in. He came to Sarah; she was seated in a garden-chair waiting bravely for him. He stood in front of her. 'I've come to know your mind once for all.'

'I think you know my mind,' she said, gently, ' and I'm sure you know my heart.'

' No, Sarah, I don't, not to the bottom.'

' Perhaps not. Women-folk were always hard for men to understand. Never heed that. Speak your own mind to me, dear Joseph.'

And Pinder said he was there on purpose. ' But first,' said he, ' let me put a question to you. I'm almost ashamed to, though.'

' It is no time to be afraid or ashamed,' said she, solemnly. ' Let me know all that is in your heart—the heart that I am losing.'

' No, no,' said Pinder, ' not if you think it worth keeping. Well, Sarah, what I am driven to ask you is : what can any man do to earn a woman more than I have done? I have loved you honestly these ten years. I was true to you when you didn't belong to me. I tried to serve your husband for your sake—a chap I always disliked and despised. You found him out at last, and parted with him. Then I hid my mind no longer.'

' It never was hidden from me.'

' Since you came back alone I have courted you openly. You don't forbid me. You almost seem to return my love.'

' Almost seem! I love you with all my heart and soul. I never loved as I love you, for I never esteemed.'

' Ah! If I could only believe that ! '

' You may believe it. I never told a lie. -My heart turned to you when I saw you in my dream, and thought of your long fidelity and no reward. My poor Joseph, my heart turned more and more to you as the ship sailed homeward, and you were the one that made coming home seem sweetest to me. Where are your eyes? Since I came home have I ever regretted the creature I used to pine for?' (She put her white hands to her face, and blushed.) ' Women don't *make* love as men do, but they *show* it in more ways than men do, to those who will but see it.'

'Then show me a little love—real love. Make me your husband!'

'How can I?'

'Easy enough. Divorce that villain, and marry me. It is a plain case of desertion and infidelity. You can get a divorce for the asking.'

'What! Go to law?'

'Why not? It's done every day by your betters.'

She coloured faintly, and said with gentle dignity, 'My superiors, you mean. They do a many things I can't, besides painting and powdering of their faces. Me go to a court of law to part those that were joined till death in a church? That I could never do.'

Pinder got angry. He belonged to a debating club, and he let her have it accordingly. 'That is all superstition. The priests used to tell ignorant folks that marriage was a sacrament, and only the Pope of Rome could annul

it. But we are not slaves of superstition and
priestcraft nowadays. Marriage is not a sacrament; it is a contract, no more, no less. Your
husband has broken it contrary to law, and you
have only got to dissolve it according to law.
Wouldn't I divorce a faithless wife for you?
And you would do as much for me, if you
loved me as I love you.'

'I love you better,' said she; 'by the same
token, I couldn't quarrel with you as you do
with me. Oh! pray, pray don't ask me to go
into a public court, and say I only come to be
freed from a wicked husband, and then have
to own another man is waiting to take me.
Ah! if you respected me as I do you, you
couldn't—'

'I have respected you these ten years, and
I've shown it. Now it is time to respect myself.
I'm the laughing-stock of my friends for my
calf-love.'

'Ah!' cried she in dismay, 'if they have
been and wounded your vanity, it is all over.
A man's love cannot stand against his vanity.

But oh ! if they knew how you are loved and
respected, they would be ashamed to play upon
you so.   Dear Joseph, be patient, as I am.
Believe that I love you better than you or any
man born can ever love me.   You are so agitated
and so angry, you frighten me, dear.   Do but
think calmly one moment : what is the best
thing in holy wedlock, after all ?   Is it not the
respect, and the tender affection, and the sweet
company ?   What husband is more cherished
than you, or better loved ?   My sister loves
you ; my child loves you ; I love you dearly.
If you could but see us when you are away,
how dead-alive the place is, and we all sit mum-
chance ; but the moment you come we are
all gay and talkative.   You are our master, our
delight, our very sunshine, and is *that* nothing ? '

Joseph Pinder drank the honey with glisten-
ing eyes, but he could not quite digest it.   He
said these were sweet words, and there was a
time when they would have charmed his ears,
and blinded him to the hard truth.   But he
was older now, and had learned that woman's

words are air. It is only by her actions you
can ever know her heart.

'James Mansell,' he said, 'is a man of my
age. 'Tisn't likely we shall both outlive him.
So when you say you will not divorce him, that
is as much as to say you will never be my wife
till he is so obliging as to die. What is that
but treating me like a calf? I won't die a
bachelor to please James Mansell, nor any
woman that clings to him *for life.* I will leave
this, kill or cure.'

Sarah objected firmly to that: 'No, Joseph,
if we are to part, it is for me to go and you to
stay. This pretty house and garden I have
enjoyed so, 'tis the fruit of your industry, and
your skill, and your affection, that I cannot
recompense as you require, and so you will
call me ungrateful some day, and break my
heart altogether. My dear, you must oblige
me in this one thing, you must live here, and
send me back to my little shop, and let me see
you get rich, and make some woman happy
that will love you better than I do. You

loved me most when I stood at that little counter in Green Street, and didn't even pretend to be a lady.' She began steadily enough, but, with all her resolution, her voice failed, and she ended in tears.

' No, Sarah, you are not going to get it all your own way. Lucy loves me, and would be my daughter to-morrow. I won't hurt her; and I could not let you go back to Green Street. I'll take nothing with me but my carpet-bag, and my pride, and the heart you have worn out.'

Then Sarah began to cry in earnest :

' Oh, Joseph,' said she, in accents to melt a stone, ' is it not sorrow enough to part? Can you part in anger ? I wouldn't be angry with *you* if you were to kill me.'

' Part in anger? ' said he. ' Heaven forbid ! Forgive me, my darling, if I have spoken a harsh word ; and give me your hand at parting.' He put out his hand, she seized it, and kissed it passionately. He kissed hers as tenderly, and their tears fell fast upon each other's hands. But he was a man, and had said he would go. So he actually did tear himself away, and catch up his bag, and through the wicket-gate; and such was his manly resolution and his wounded pride that he went thirty—or at least twenty-five—yards before he wished himself back upon any terms whatever. Till now he never knew how much she loved him.

As for Sarah, she did not attempt to deceive herself or any one else. She laid her brow on the little table, and sobbed piteously. Deborah came running to her, and took off her bonnet the first thing, for why should she spoil that as well as break her heart? But while saving the sacred bonnet, she was trying to comfort the heart.

'How could he leave you? How could you let him? It will kill you.'

'Perhaps not. I trust in Heaven.'

'Don't cry like that, dear,' sobbed Deborah. 'He will come back in a month or two, and then you will give in to him.'

'No. I can only cry for him, and trust in my Redeemer, as I did when that creature played me false. I didn't trust in vain. Bring me my child.'

Deborah put Lucy on her lap, and Sarah fondled her and cried over her. Presently what should Deborah see but Joseph Pinder at the wicket-gate with his bag. She ran to him all in a hurry and whispered, 'Not yet, ye foolish—you mustn't come back for a week; then she will be like wax.'

'I'm not coming back at all,' said Pinder, loud and aggressively. 'It is only out of civility. Lady and gentleman from America looking everywhere for her.' Then he held the gate open, and beckoned to a lady and gentleman. They appeared, and at his invitation passed through the wicket.

Now Sarah had ears like a hare. She heard every word, and her smile of celestial love and just a little earthly triumph at Pinder's voice and self-deception was delicious; only, as she had been crying, she could not face these visitors all in a moment, but dried her eyes and tried to compose her features. Just then Pinder pointed her out in silence, and Solomon Grace walked gravely down the garden, and drew up stiffly at her right hand. Mrs. Grace also moved toward Sarah, but hung back a little. There was an air of solemnity about them both. Pinder, instead of retiring again, crept down a little way with his bag, and a swift exchange of words passed between him and Deborah.

'You came out of civility: what are you staying for?'

'Curiosity,' snarled Pinder.

As soon as Mrs. Mansell saw Solomon Grace she said, eagerly, 'Oh, my good friend, you here? Welcome!' She put out both hands to him.

He took them, and said, gravely, 'We bring you serious news.'

At the sound 'we,' Sarah turned, and there was Mrs. Grace. She welcomed her just as she had done her husband. Lucy made a school

curtsey to both of them.   There was a hesitation.   Grace and his wife looked at each other.

'Yes, you can tell her,' said Elizabeth.

Sarah Mansell eyed them keenly.   'Yes,
you can tell me : whoever is false to me is
dead to me from that moment.'   She half
divined the truth.   Some women can read
faces, manner, incidents, all in a moment, and
put them together.   This was one.

'Yes,' said Elizabeth, 'I am glad you are
prepared for it.   James Mansell is no more.'

Then Grace handed her the certificate of
Mansell's death.

Mrs. Grace resumed : 'He died in the hospital, and he died penitent, begging forgiveness
of those he had injured.   Mrs. Mansell, I stood
by his bedside and pardoned him.'

'And so do I,' said Sarah.   'I forgive him
with all my heart, as I hope to be one day
forgiven ;' and she raised her pious eyes to
heaven.

Whilst this was going on, Deborah came
behind Pinder, who was listening gravely to

every word, and quietly took the bag away out of his hand, and then his hat; both of these she handed to the servant-girl, and bade her hide them. Susan took the hint in a moment. Thus disarmed, Joseph sat meekly down in a chair at some distance, and Lucy immediately seated herself on his knee, with an arm round his neck. Sarah parted for the present with her American friends, but took their address, and in due course entertained them hospitably.

But this was a solemn day, and though she scorned to feign a single particle of regret, yet she felt it was not a day for conviviality. When she had bidden the Graces 'good-bye' at the wicket-gate, she walked slowly toward the house. Then, looking askant, her eye fell on Pinder, with Lucy on his knee. She stopped and looked at them. Just then the servant came out into the porch and announced dinner. Sarah smiled sweetly on the pair, and said, ' Come, my dears.'

They both came; Joseph very humbly. But Sarah never uttered one syllable of comment on his temporary revolt.   He, on his part, tried his best to make her forget their one quarrel.   But that was quite unnecessary, and she let him see it.   She never thought him in the wrong, but only thought herself in the right, and she never showed him even the shadow of resentment or exultation.   She was ' Singleheart,' and she loved him.

When, after waiting a decent time, he threw out a timid hint that he hoped he might call her his own before so very long, she opened her eyes, and said, ' *Whenever you please, dear. I'm only waiting your pleasure.*'   He was amazed.   But that did not prevent his catching her to him with rapture.

In the ardent colloquy that followed this embrace he said he had been fearing she would demand a year's delay.

' Not I,' said she ; ' nor yet a month's.   To be sure, I have my own old-fashioned notions of *decency*; but when it comes to ceremony, I would not set up such straws against *you*, not for one moment.   What is etiquette to me?

I am not a lady.' [I am not so sure of that as she was.]

So they were married off-hand, and she soon showed Joe Pinder whether she loved him or not. All he had ever dreamed of love never came near hers. His happiness is perfect; and ten times the sweeter that he waited for it, pined for it, lost it entirely, earned it again, gained it by halves, then enjoyed it to the full.

To the world they are just thriving traders, very diligent and square in business, but benevolent; yet their private history is more romantic than the lives of nineteen poets in twenty.

Deborah is courting diligently. One Sunday afternoon Lucy, nodding over a good book, yet fitfully observant, saw her wooed by three eligible parties in turn over the palings. Then Lucy asked her which she was going to marry.

' How can I tell? ' said she.

' Are they all three so very nice ? ' inquired Lucy, slily.

'They are all three nicer than none at all,' was Deborah's reply.

LUCY'S LAST.

'Aunt Deb, I don't think you will ever be married.'

'That's good news for me. And why not?'

'Because marriages are made in *heaven.*'

Now it is not for me to predict the future; but from my observations of the Lucy Mansells I have known, I should expect to find that young lady at seventeen excessively modest and retiring, but as stupid as an owl.

www.ingramcontent.com/pod-product-compliance
Lightning Source LLC
Chambersburg PA
CBHW020856270326
41928CB00006B/735